microwaving meals in 30 minutes

microwave cooking library™

by barbara methven

How fast is fast? Microwave cooking has many advantages: juicy meats and poultry, fresh tasting vegetables, higher, more tender cakes, energy savings and easy clean up, but microwave speed is still one of the main benefits of a microwave oven.

Many microwave oven owners would like to microwave a meal in about half an hour. Some would be willing to add a few extra minutes to microwave a special side dish or dessert, while others would cut the time even more by serving canned vegetables and fresh fruit with a main dish which takes only 15 minutes to cook.

This book is designed to show you how to make fast microwave meals even faster. The emphasis is on main dishes (cooking times range from about 10 minutes to 30 minutes). To complete the meal, you add a starch, vegetable, salad, even a dessert, to suit your tastes and your time schedule.

Microwaving Meals in 30 Minutes tells you how to save time in planning, marketing and preparing a meal. With good time management, you can serve a satisfying meal in 20 minutes, or a feast in less than an hour.

Barbara Methven

Barbara Methven

CREDITS:

Design & Production: Cy DeCosse Creative Department, Inc.
Author: Barbara Methven
Home Economists: Jill Crum, Carol Grones, Peggy Lamb, Cynthia Sampson
Food Stylists: Akiko Yamamoto, Maria Rolandelli, Kathy Lucas, Janna Arnold
Photographers: Michael Jensen, Steven Smith, Jack Mithun
Production Coordinators: Julia Slott Lindeberg, Bernice Maehren, Nancy McDonough, Stuart Smith, Mary Sweet
Consumer Testers: Robyn Cook, Sue Lowenberg, Judith Richard, Julia Slott Lindeberg
Color Separations: Weston Engraving Co., Inc.
Printing: Moebius Printing Co.

Contents

What You Need to Know Before You Start

The secret of fast and efficient meal preparation is time management. Even when you have only half an hour to make dinner, you can plan your time to make the most of every minute without being flurried. Good time management involves three activities: Menu planning, grocery shopping and food preparation.

Plan Ahead

When cooking time is limited, it's important to have your menu planned in advance. Every moment you spend paging through the cookbook or deciding what to cook cuts down the time you have left to cook it.

Plan menus for several days, or even a week at a time. Consult your supermarket's advertised specials for meat, fish, poultry or produce. Check your freezer for foods you may want to use during the week.

List the type of protein you wish to serve at each meal, then select main dish recipes for them. Many of the main dishes in this book include a complementary vegetable or starch, so you can cook two foods at once.

Plan the other components of the meal at the same time. Vary the menus by selecting different starches, vegetables, salads or desserts for each day. Take advantage of frozen or canned fruits, convenience foods, pickles, and other items which can round out a meal without consuming preparation time.

Suit Yourself

This book offers sample menus to help you get started. It demonstrates how the same main dish can be used for several menus to provide flexibility and variety. Your meal plans will reflect your individual tastes and needs if you keep these four things in mind.

Balanced Nutrition. Speedy meals can be just as nutritious as the ones which take hours to prepare. In fact, many foods benefit from quick cooking because they retain more vitamins and minerals.

Family Tastes. Some families avoid starches and desserts, while others feel a meal is not complete without them.

The Occasion. Saturday supper and Sunday dinner call for different menus. If you're entertaining guests, you may want to serve an appetizer. This book includes main dishes for fast party fare.

Your Time. On very busy days, you may want a vegetable which cooks in three minutes. With more time to spare, you might select one which takes ten.

Shop Ahead

A visit to the supermarket takes time. Make the best use of your marketing time by shopping once a week with an efficient grocery list. As you plan your menus, jot down all the ingredients you will need. Group them by sections in the store: meat, produce, dairy case, canned goods, or frozen foods. Add to the list any staples that are running low or items you want to stock for emergencies. Avoid shopping during the rush hour, so you won't have a long wait in the check-out line.

Ready...Set...Go

Start with food which has the longest standing time. None of these recipes requires more than 5 to 10 minutes standing, but most of the main dishes can be held longer when properly covered.

If something on the menu takes a good deal of preliminary chopping or mixing, microwave another food first. Use that cooking time for preparation.

When a food requires stirring or rotating during cooking, set your timer so the bell will remind you. Get the second food ready while the first is cooking.

While the first food is standing and the second is cooking, you might toss a salad, set the table, or prepare a dessert to microwave while the family is eating dinner. If you're serving rolls, warm them briefly at the last minute.

How to Make the Most of Your Time

The meat or main dish is the most important part of the meal, but it doesn't have to be time-consuming to prepare. Most recipes in this book microwave in 10 to 30 minutes. To save even more time at the last minute, read the recipe the night before. Take a few minutes to make sure you have the ingredients needed, marinate the meat, do some advance preparation, plan side dishes which will cook in the time you have to spare.

Prepare some ingredients in the morning or the night before. Chop or slice vegetables; cook and crumble bacon. If a casserole calls for white sauce or a topping of mashed potatoes, it can be microwaved and refrigerated overnight, then reheated before use.

Pound and marinate meat for "overnight" recipes as soon as you buy it. Marinating several days in the refrigerator makes meat more tender and flavorful.

Speed preparation of ingredients by using time-saving appliances, such as a food processor, mixer attachments or electric slicer.

Cook pasta or rice on your conventional range while you microwave the main dish. You may even have time to microwave a vegetable or dessert while the starch cooks.

Use the standing time of a meat or casserole to microwave a vegetable or side dish to go with it. To hold food even longer, cover tightly or wrap in foil or plastic wrap.

Microwave a quick dessert while the family eats dinner. Heat sauce for a sundae, or defrost frozen fruit or cake.

How to Make Speedy Meals Even Faster

Almost anything you cook will be faster in a microwave oven than it is conventionally. The main dishes in this book were selected because most of them take less than 30 minutes of microwave time. However, actual cooking time is only part of the story; preparation takes time, too. The speed with which a meal can be on the table depends on your own pace, work habits, and the state of your kitchen. If you have to clear off a counter before you can start, that adds to the time. The following suggestions will help cut minutes off preparation.

Plan meals in advance, and check to make sure you have the ingredients needed. Searching through cookbooks when you could be starting dinner consumes valuable time.

Collect ingredients and utensils before you start to cook. Use microwave oven-to-table ware. You'll save the time needed to transfer food to serving dishes, and clean-up time, too.

Prepare some ingredients the night before or in the morning. With some meals, chopping

What to Keep In Your Pantry

Dry products
Bread crumbs
Bread sticks
Buttermilk baking mix
Corn flake crumbs
Cornstarch
Flavored rice mixes
Graham cracker crumbs
Herb stuffing mix
Instant bouillon granules
Instant mashed potatoes
Instant minced onion
One-layer cake mixes
Parsley flakes
Quick-cooking rice
Soup and gravy mixes
Staples (flour, sugar, etc.)

Bottled & canned goods
Beef bouillon
Bouquet sauce
Chicken broth
Crab
Cream soups
Dry sherry or vermouth
Evaporated milk
Kidney or garbanzo beans
Miscellaneous vegetables
Mushrooms
Olive and salad oil
Onion rings
Salmon
Shoe string potatoes
Shrimp
Soy sauce
Stewed tomatoes
Sweetened condensed milk
Tomato paste
Tomato sauce
Tuna
Water chestnuts
Worcestershire sauce

and slicing takes more time than cooking.

Use your freezer. Defrosting ingredients adds to preparation time, but doesn't take as long as a last-minute trip to the supermarket. When buying meat for the freezer, make sure there are no ice crystals in it. These indicate that meat has already been frozen once.

Freeze leftovers in ready-to-use form and quantity. Label them with the name of the recipe for which they were prepared.

Make double batches of spaghetti sauce, chili, or your favorite casseroles when you have the time. Freeze the extra portions in individual servings for quick defrosting and heating.

Keep a well-stocked pantry, freezer and refrigerator. With the following list, you can make many of the recipes in this book, as well as some quick side dishes and desserts. Stocking up can be expensive. To spread the cost, buy a few items each time you shop, then replace items as you use them.

What to Keep in Your Freezer & Refrigerator

Freezer
- Appetizer sausages
- Chicken parts
- Chopped green pepper
- Corn on the cob
- Fish fillets
- Freeze-dried chives
- Fruits
- Ground beef in flat, recipe-size packages
- Mushrooms
- Pie shells
- Pork chops in individual heat-sealable bags
- Potato tots
- Prepared meat mixes from this book
- Vegetables in poly bags
- Whipped topping

Refrigerator
- Bacon
- Barbecue sauce
- Bottled lemon juice
- Canned ham
- Carrots
- Catsup
- Celery
- Chili sauce
- Cream cheese
- Eggs
- Grated cheeses
- Green pepper
- Horseradish sauce
- Milk
- Onions
- Prepared mustard
- Process cheese spread
- Shredded cheeses

How to Plan Meals From This Book

Busy people who skip breakfast or snack at noon, need well-balanced nutrition at dinner. Plan meals which include the "basic four": meat (including poultry, fish, eggs or cheese), milk (used in cooking or served as a beverage), vegetables and fruit, cereals or starchy vegetables.

Start with the main dish, which provides complete protein. The main dishes in this book have been divided into three sections, based on preparation and microwaving time. Select one which fits your schedule.

Choose complements that will balance nutrition, round out the meal, and still fit into your remaining time.

Vegetables. Some of the main dishes include a vegetable which is microwaved at the same time as the meat or fish. A vegetable section provides quick recipes, plus instructions for frozen and canned vegetables. A salad of lettuce or fruit can be prepared while the main dish is cooking.

Cereals and starches. These supply important food elements and satisfy hunger. They can be pasta or rice, canned legumes (dried beans or peas), potatoes, corn or winter squash, or simply bread and rolls, which take no cooking time. If you're dieting, serve them without fats, rich sauces, or jams and jellies.

Appetizers and desserts. These are nice to serve, although not essential. For some people, they make the difference between a snack and a real dinner, and can be used to balance nutrition. Try one of our quick recipes, or serve an appetizer of raw vegetables or cheese and crackers, and a dessert of fruit, pudding or ice cream.

How to Plan and Microwave a Meal to Suit Your Time

Both these menus start with the same main dish, Chicken Breasts with Wine and Mushrooms. If the chicken was boned by the butcher, it can be ready for the table in under 20 minutes. The time difference between the two menus is due to the meal complements. For both menus, preparation and microwaving time are managed efficiently.

#1 When You're in a Hurry

Chicken Breasts with Wine and Mushrooms, page 56	10¼ to 14¾ min.
Waldorf Salad	
Canned peas, page 143	2 to 3 min.
6 to 8 rolls, warm	¼ to ¾ min.
Ice Cream with Mint Chocolate Sauce, page 151	1 to 2½ min.
Total:	13½ min. to 21 min.

#2 When You Have More Time

Chicken Breasts with Wine and Mushrooms, page 56	10¼ to 14¾ min.
Zucchini Parmesan, page 140	4 to 6 min.
Baked Potatoes, page 132	10½ to 12½ min.
Marinated Tomato Wedges	
Cherry Almond Torte, page 151	3 to 4 min.
Total:	27¾ to 37¼ min.

How to Microwave Menu #1

Melt butter for wine sauce. Wash and slice mushrooms; add to chicken and start microwaving while mixing sauce. Drain peas and place in serving dish.

Add wine sauce to chicken; cook while preparing salad and combining ingredients for dessert sauce.

Heat peas, then rolls, while chicken stands, covered. Microwave dessert sauce while dishing ice cream and clearing table.

How to Microwave Menu #2

Microwave potatoes. Cut tomatoes in wedges; sprinkle with garlic dressing. Set aside. Combine chicken and mushrooms.

Wrap potatoes in foil and let stand. While main dish cooks, slice zucchini and mix topping.

Microwave zucchini while you assemble torte to heat just before serving.

Sample Dinners

These menus show how you can prepare a balanced meal using the recipes in this book and adding salads, breads or fruits. Microwaving times range from 15½ to 32½ minutes. The samples explain how to minimize additional preparation time by microwaving one dish while you mix another.

Bacon-Wrapped Mini Meatloaves, page 26	12 to 15½ min.
Instant Mashed Potatoes, page 132	4 to 7 min.
Canned Green Beans, page 142	2 to 4 min.
Sliced Tomatoes	
Canned Peach Halves Topped with Ice Cream and Sliced Almonds	

Total: 18 to 26½ min.

Microwave chopped vegetables and bacon. Mix and shape meatloaves while heating water for potatoes. Set potatoes aside, lightly covered. Microwave meatloaves, then heat beans while meatloaves are standing.

Pork Chops with Creamy Rice & Peas, page 113	25 to 30 min.
Assorted Pickles or Spiced Apple Rings	
Tossed Green Salad	
Pound Cake with Fresh Strawberries & Whipped Cream	

Total: 25 to 30 min.

Defrost pound cake at room temperature. While microwaving main dish, clean berries, whip cream and refrigerate.

Pepper Steak Strips, page 107	21 to 26½ min.
Rice, cooked conventionally	
Alfalfa Sprout Salad	
Orange Ice with Fortune Cookies	

Total: 21 to 26½ min.

Cook rice conventionally. Prepare and season meat. Slice and chop vegetables while preheating browning dish.

Ham & Cheese Filled Cabbage Rolls, page 43 — 6½ to 11 min.
Boiled Potato Quarters
Dill Pickles & Radishes
Combination Salad
Melon Boats with Sherbert

Total: 15½ to 23 min.

Soften cabbage leaves. Microwave potatoes while preparing cabbage rolls. Let potatoes stand, covered, while microwaving main dish.

Lemon-Dill Veal, page 39 — 9¾ to 11¾ min.
Flavored rice, cooked conventionally
Frozen Broccoli Spears, page 142 — 8 to 10 min.
Tomato & Cucumber Salad
Cheesecake with Strawberry Sauce, page 151 — 3¼ to 4 min.

Total: 21 to 25¾ min.

Cook rice conventionally. Partially defrost cheesecake. Microwave broccoli, let stand tightly covered while cooking veal. Heat topping while slicing cheesecake.

Stroganoff from Make-Ahead Mix, page 88 — 11½ to 18½ min.
Noodles, cooked conventionally
Frozen Cauliflowerets, page 142 — 8 to 10 min.
Pickled Beets on Lettuce Cups
Cherry Almond Torte, page 152 — 3 to 4 min.

Total: 22½ to 32½ min.

Cook noodles conventionally. Defrost mix, then microwave cauliflower and set aside, covered, while finishing main dish and assembling dessert to heat just before serving.

Chicken on Scalloped Corn, page 52 — 20 to 25 min.
Frozen Pea Pods, page 143 — 5 to 6 min.
Celery & Carrot Sticks, Olives
Fresh Fruit

Total: 25 to 31 min.

Microwave chicken and corn. Set aside while cooking pea pods.

Fast But Fancy Dinners

Dinner for guests or a special occasion need not take hours of work in the kitchen. To simplify last-minute preparation, many of the desserts in these menus are microwaved the night before, or while the guests are eating dinner. They are included in the total microwaving time, which is about 30 minutes or less.

Veal in Sour Cream, page 39	7¼ to 9¼ min.
Noodles, cooked conventionally	
Frozen Broccoli Spears, page 142	8 to 12 min.
Sliced Cucumbers with Dill	
Pound Cake with Lemon-Orange Sauce, page 151	2 to 4 min.
	Total: 17¼ to 25¼ min.

Start noodles and make dessert sauce first. Microwave broccoli; hold tightly covered while cooking veal. Defrost cake at room temperature while guests are eating dinner.

Shrimp in Buttery Sauce, page 63	5 to 8½ min.
Piquant Pecans, page 145	8 to 12½ min.
Rice, cooked conventionally	
Zucchini & Tomatoes, page 140	4 to 6 min.
Boston Lettuce with Oil and Vinegar Dressing	
Overnight Cranberry Ice Cream Pie, page 152	2¾ to 3½ min.
	Total: 19¾ to 30½ min.

Prepare dessert the night before. Pecans may be microwaved in advance or at the time you start the rice. Do zucchini next, then shrimp.

Crab Stuffed Chicken Breasts, page 61	6½ to 9½ min.
Fresh Corn on Cob, page 143	17 to 21 min.
Tossed Green Salad with Cherry Tomatoes	
Cheesecake with Strawberry Topping, page 151	3¼ to 4 min.
	Total: 26¾ to 34½ min.

Defrost cheesecake first. Microwave corn while stuffing chicken breasts, then hold, tightly covered, while chicken cooks. Heat strawberry sauce while clearing table.

Crab Newburg in Patty Shells, page 62 — 5½ to 10 min.
Fresh Asparagus, page 142 — 9½ to 12½ min.
Fruit Salad with Honey Dressing

Total: 15 to 22½ min.

Bake patty shells conventionally. Prepare Newburg sauce, let stand while microwaving asparagus. Add crab to sauce and heat just before serving.

Glazed Ham & Sweet Potatoes, page 42 — 8 to 11 min.
Italian Brussels Sprouts, page 136 — 9 to 11½ min.
Sliced Tomato Salad
Hot Fruit Compote, page 152 — 6½ to 8 min.

Total: 23½ to 30½ min.

Partially defrost peaches. Cook Brussels sprouts and onion-butter. Set aside. Microwave ham and sweet potatoes while mixing fruit compote. Reheat Brussels sprouts. Microwave dessert while guests are eating dinner.

Cornish Hens with Brazil Nut Stuffing, page 124 — 15¾ to 22¼ min.
Peas, Onions and Mushrooms, page 139 — 6½ to 8 min.
Jellied Cranberry Relish
Lettuce Cups
Rolls
Apple Turnovers (frozen)

Total: 22¼ to 30¼ min.

Bake turnovers conventionally. Microwave onion and butter for vegetables while stuffing Cornish hens. Let hens stand, covered, while finishing peas and mushrooms.

Pork Chops on Fruit & Vegetable Stuffing, page 115 — 20 to 26¼ min.
Cole Slaw
Rolls
Overnight Rocky Road Ice Cream Pie, page 152 — 2¾ to 3½ min.

Total: 22¾ to 29¾ min.

Prepare dessert the night before. Make cole slaw while microwaving pork chops.

One-Dish Dinners

These main dishes include a protein and a starch or vegetable microwaved at the same time. Complementary dishes help satisfy appetites and provide balanced nutrition.

Chicken with French Green Beans Dinner, page 59	18 to 23 min.
Instant Mashed Potatoes, made conventionally	
Spiced Peaches in Lettuce Cups	
Overnight Pumpkin Ice Cream Pie, page 152	2¾ to 3½ min.
Total:	**20¾ to 26½ min.**

Make dessert the night before. Prepare potatoes conventionally while microwaving chicken and beans.

Scallops & Green Beans, page 64	7½ to 12¼ min.
Flavored Rice, cooked conventionally	
Lettuce, Tomato & Mushroom Salad	
Hot Fruit Compote, page 152	6½ to 8 min.
Total:	**14 to 20¼ min.**

Cook rice conventionally. Defrost peaches, set aside. Microwave scallops and beans, while mixing compote to heat while family is eating dinner.

Saucy Burgers & Rice, page 28	12½ to 17½ min.
Frozen Peas, page 143	7 to 9 min.
Tomato Wedges	
Ice Cream with Peanut Butter Chocolate Sauce, page 151	1 to 3 min.
Total:	**20½ to 29½ min.**

Microwave rice and burgers; let stand, covered. Cook peas, then finish sauce while peas are standing. Microwave sundae sauce while clearing table and dishing ice cream.

Pork Chops & Stuffed Tomatoes, page 115 — 23 to 26 min.
Cole Slaw
Dark Rye Rolls
Pineapple Sherbert

Total: 23 to 26 min.

Prepare cole slaw while microwaving chops and tomatoes. To speed shredding, use a food processor.

Cubed Steaks & Brussels Sprouts Plate, page 25 — 19 to 23 min.
Instant Mashed Potatoes, page 132 — 4 to 7 min.
Tossed Salad
Oranges & Bananas Topped with Coconut

Total: 23 to 30 min.

Microwave water and butter for instant mashed potatoes while arranging cube steaks and sprouts in baking dish. After mixing potatoes, set aside, covered. Warm 1 to 2 minutes if needed, before serving.

Fish & Pepper Cups, page 66 — 6 to 9½ min.
Baked Potatoes, page 132 — 10½ to 12½ min.
Lettuce Wedges with Bottled Dressing
Canned Pears with Mint Chocolate Sauce, page 151 — 1 to 2½ min.

Total: 17½ to 24½ min.

Microwave potatoes while preparing fish and pepper cups. Wrap in foil and let stand while cooking main dish. Microwave dessert sauce while clearing the table.

Polish Sausages & Creamy Potatoes, page 47 — 11¾ to 15 min.
Lightly Glazed Carrots, page 137 — 7¾ to 9 min.
Applesauce
Ice Cream with Chocolate-Butterscotch Sauce, page 151 — 1 to 3 min.

Total: 20½ to 27 min.

Microwave potatoes and cream cheese sauce. Set aside while cooking carrots. Complete main dish, then glaze and reheat carrots, if necessary. Microwave sundae sauce while dishing ice cream.

Casserole Dinners

These tasty mixtures simplify cooking by combining protein and vegetables in one hot dish. Two of them use make-ahead mixes which you can prepare in advance and keep on hand in the freezer. While the casserole microwaves, make a salad and simple dessert to complete the meal.

Chicken Casserole from Make-Ahead Mix, page 99 — 21 to 31½ min.
Jellied Cranberry Sauce in Lettuce Cups
Pound Cake with Fresh Strawberries and Whipped Cream

Total: 21 to 31½ min.

Cook macaroni conventionally while defrosting mix and assembling casserole ingredients. While microwaving main dish, defrost cake at room temperature; prepare and refrigerate strawberries and whipped cream.

Tuna Medley, page 69 — 7½ to 11½ min.
Fresh & Canned Fruit Salad with Sweet-Sour Dressing
Hard Rolls
Ice Cream with Mint-Chocolate Sauce, page 151 — 1 to 2½ min.

Total: 8½ to 13 min.

Assemble dessert sauce and prepare salad while microwaving casserole. Heat sauce while dishing ice cream.

Taco Salad, page 36 — 14½ to 19½ min.
Corn Chips with Guacamole
Hot Fruit Compote, page 152 — 6½ to 8 min.

Total: 21 to 27½ min.

Defrost peaches; set aside while preparing main dish. Heat compote while family is eating dinner.

Ham & Zucchini in Cheese Sauce, page 42 — 10½ to 17½ min.
Noodles, cooked conventionally
Lettuce & Tomato Salad
Peaches with Frozen Raspberries — 1 to 3 min.

Total: 11½ to 20½ min.

Cook noodles conventionally. Partially defrost pouch of frozen raspberries; set aside until serving time. Microwave Ham & Zucchini sauce.

Pork Chop Suey from Make-Ahead Mix, page 93 — 18 to 25½ min.
Tossed Salad with Chives, Fresh Grapefruit & Mandarin Oranges
Pound Cake with Peanut Butter Chocolate Sauce, page 151 — 1 to 3 min.

Total: 19 to 28½ min.

Prepare grapefruit segments and mix dessert sauce while microwaving casserole. Defrost pound cake while family is eating dinner. Microwave sauce just before serving.

Mexican Lasagna, page 74 — 19 to 27 min.
Shredded Lettuce Salad with Chopped Avocado, Tomato & Black olives
Cherry Almond Torte, page 152 — 3 to 4 min.

Total: 22 to 31 min.

Mix filling while microwaving onion mixture. Assemble salad and torte while microwaving casserole. Heat torte while main dish is standing.

Wieners & Sauerkraut, page 50 — 9 to 14 min.
Baked Potatoes, page 132 — 10½ to 12½ min.
Spinach Salad
Lime Sherbert

Total: 19½ to 26½ min.

Microwave potatoes while preparing ingredients for casserole, then wrap in foil and let stand.

Meal/Time Planning Chart

Use this chart to help you plan menus. Main Dishes and Complements are listed according to the time they take to microwave. Don't forget to add a little more time for preparation.

	8 Minutes or Less	9-15 Minutes
Beef		Overnight Marinated Teriyaki Strips, page 106
Ground Beef		Bacon Stuffed Patties with Mushrooms & Onions, page 29 Bacon-Wrapped Mini Meatloaves, page 26 Chili, page 88 Hamburger Quiche, page 36 Individual Mexican Meatloaves, page 27 Meatballs & Baked Beans, page 31 Meatballs with Potatoes & Carrots, page 110 Meatballs on Rice, page 110 Oriental Meatloaves, page 27 Saucy Burgers & Rice, page 28 Stroganoff, page 88 Taco Salad, page 36
Ham	Gingered Ham Kabobs, page 41 Glazed Ham & Sweet Potatoes, page 42 Ham & Cheese Filled Cabbage Rolls, page 43	Ham & Zucchini in Cheese Sauce, page 42
Lamb		Lamb Burgers, page 45 Lamb Creole, page 45 Lamb Meatballs with Dill Sauce, page 44 Overnight Marinated Lamb Kabobs, page 117
Pork		Pork Schnitzel, page 40
Sausage	Bologna Kabobs, page 51 Open Face Cheese Dogs, page 50	Cabbage Rolls, page 118 Company Macaroni, Sausage & Cheese, page 49 Link Sausage & Cheesy Potatoes, page 48 Polish Sausages & Creamy Potatoes, page 47 Polynesian Bean & Wiener Bake, page 47 Sausage & Spinach Noodle Casserole, page 118 Texas Cornbread Casserole, page 51 Wieners & Sauerkraut, page 50
Veal		Lemon-Dill Veal, page 39 Veal Parmigiana, page 38

16-20 Minutes	21-25 Minutes	26-30 Minutes
Cubed Steaks & Brussels Sprouts Plate, page 25 Swiss Cubed Steaks, page 24	Beef Strips in Tomato Sauce, page 106 Cubed Steaks on a Bed of Vegetables, pg. 24 Overnight Marinated West Coast Round Steak, page 104 Pepper Steak Strips, page 107	Overnight Marinated Stuffed Flank Steak, pg. 105
Beef & Beans with Dumplings, page 30 Hamburger Stew, page 31 Shepherds Pie, page 32 Sweet & Sour Meatballs, page 111	Basic Beef Mix, page 86 Chili Rice, page 33 Four-Layer Dinner, page 109 Spaghetti Beef Mix, page 87 Stuffed Green Peppers, page 91	Italian Meatloaf, page 108 Lasagna, page 89 Layered Casserole, page 90
Barbecued Lamb Chops, page 116 Orange Glazed Lamb Chops, page 116		Lamb Stew, page 117
Barbecue Pork Chops, page 41 Pork Chop Suey, page 93 Pork & Sauerkraut, page 93	Pork Chops with Creamy Rice & Peas, page 113 Pork Chops on Fruit & Vegetable Stuffing, page 115 Pork Chops & Saucy Vegetables, page 113 Pork Chop, Sauerkraut & Potatoes, page 113 Pork Chops & Stuffed Tomatoes, page 115 Pork & Refried Bean Enchiladas, page 94 Stuffed Pork Chops & Brussels Sprout Dinner, page 114	Basic Pork Mix, page 92
	Wurst & German Potato Salad, page 119	
	Veal in Sour Cream, page 39	

Meal/Time Planning Chart (continued)

	8 Minutes or Less	9-15 Minutes
Chicken	Company Chicken Breasts, page 60 Crab-Stuffed Chicken Breasts, page 61	Chicken Breasts with Wine & Mushrooms, page 60 Chicken Paprikash, page 101 Chicken & Spinach Stir-Fry, page 56 Smoky Barbecued Drumsticks, page 58
Cornish Game Hens		Cornish Hens with Brazil Nut Stuffing, page 124
Turkey		
Fish & Seafood	Crab Newburg, page 62 Crabmeat Canoes, page 62 Fish & Pepper Cups, page 66 Poached Fish & Mushrooms, page 67 Saucy Stuffed Fillets, page 67 Scallops & Green Beans, page 64 Shrimp in Buttery Sauce, page 63 Stuffed Trout, page 64 Tuna Medley, page 69	Salmon Ring, page 68 Sweet & Sour Fillets, page 66 Torsk Au Gratin, page 65 Tuna & Shrimp Casserole, page 69
Eggs & Cheese	Denver Sandwiches, page 72 Spanish Scrambled Eggs, page 72	Macaroni & Cheese, page 73 Spaghetti Carbonara, page 73 Swiss Eggs, page 75
Sandwiches	Ham or Beef Open Face Barbecue Sandwiches, page 83 Tuna-Cheese Open Face Sandwich, page 83	
Soups		Beef & Vegetable Soup, page 81 Easy Split Pea Soup, page 77 Leftover Chicken & Noodle Soup, page 79 Tomato, Hamburger & Rice Soup, page 80
Starches	Baked Potatoes, page 132 Instant Mashed Potatoes, page 132 Quick-Cooking Rice, page 132	Scalloped Hash Browns, page 134 Twice Baked Potatoes, page 133
Vegetables	Caraway Cabbage, page 137 Creamed Spinach, page 139 Harvard Beets, page 135 Lightly Glazed Carrots, page 137 Peas, Onions & Mushrooms, page 139 Zucchini Parmesan, page 140 Zucchini & Tomatoes, page 140	Cheesy Broccoli & Cauliflower, page 136 Italian Brussels Sprouts, page 136 Snapped Up Green Beans, page 135 Stir-Fried Vegetables, page 141 Stuffed Tomatoes, page 71
Appetizers	Cheese & Sausage Nuggets, page 146 Crab Balls, page 147 Make-Ahead Cheese Nuggets, page 145 Make-Ahead Piquant Pecans, page 145 Rarebit Appetizer, page 148	Cheesy Tomato Puffs, page 149 Hot Florentine Dip, page 148 Overnight Marinated Sweet & Sour Wings, page 146
Desserts	Cherry Almond Torte, page 152 Hot Fruit Compote, page 152 Lemon-Orange Sauce, page 151 Mint Chocolate Sundae, page 151 Overnight Ice Cream Pies, page 152 Peanut Butter Chocolate Sauce, page 151 Strawberry Sauce, page 151	

16-20 Minutes	21-25 Minutes	26-30 Minutes
Chicken & Broccoli Plate, page 120 Chicken in Creamy Tomato Sauce, page 54 Chicken with French Green Beans Dinner, page 59 Chicken & Mushroom Stuffing, page 122 Chicken on Scalloped Corn, page 52 Cranberry-Orange Chicken, page 53 Orange-Walnut Chicken, page 55 Quick Chicken Pilaf, page 97 Souper Chicken, page 55	Chicken & Broccoli Over Spaghetti, page 100 Chicken Casserole, page 99 Chicken & Rice, page 52 Chicken Sauced with Peas & Carrots, page 120	Basic Chicken Mix, page 96 Chicken with Sour Cream & Chive Potatoes, page 121 Chicken Stew with Dumplings, page 98
Cranberry Cornish Hens, page 125		Bacon-Stuffed Cornish Hens, page 124
	Apricot Glazed Turkey Legs, page 123	
Shrimp Creole, page 63		
Egg Foo Yung, page 128 Manicotti, page 35	Dutch Omelet, page 127 Mexican Lasagna, page 74 Overnight Cheese Stratas, page 129 Spinach Lasagna, page 34	
Chili Burgers, page 82		
Beefy Spaghetti Soup, page 81 New England Clam Chowder, page 76	Hamburger-Vegetable Soup, page 79	Creamy Beef & Sausage Soup, page 78
		Bacon-Cheese Stuffed Potatoes, page 133
	Broccoli Quiche, page 70 Riviera Eggplant Bake, page 138 Sweet Potato Puff, page 70	Mushroom Spaghetti, page 134

VAN BUREN

30 Minute Meals

30 Minute Meals

The main dishes in this section are so quick to make that you can do all the preparation and microwaving in less than half an hour. You should also have time to microwave a vegetable or make a dessert or an appetizer from the Meal Complements chapter.

Swiss Cubed Steaks

- 1 small onion, chopped
- ¼ cup chopped green pepper
- 1 can (8 oz.) tomato sauce
- 1 teaspoon instant beef bouillon granules
- 1 teaspoon Worcestershire sauce
- ½ teaspoon seasoned salt
- 4 beef cubed steaks, approx. 1¼ lb.
- ¼ cup flour

Serves 4

Place onion and green pepper in 12×8-in. baking dish. Cover with wax paper. Microwave at High 1½ to 2½ minutes, or until tender.

Stir in tomato sauce, bouillon granules, Worcestershire sauce and seasoned salt. Dredge cubed steaks in flour.

Add steaks to sauce mixture, spooning sauce over steaks to cover. Cover with wax paper. Microwave 3 minutes. Reduce power to 50% (Medium). Microwave 10 to 15 minutes, or until meat has lost its pink color, turning steaks over and rearranging after half the cooking time. Let stand 3 to 5 minutes.

Microwave	14½-20½ min.
Standing	3-5 min.

Cubed Steaks on a Bed of Vegetables ►

- 3 cups thinly sliced potatoes
- 2 cups thinly sliced carrots
- 1 can (10½ oz.) vegetable beef soup
- 4 cubed steaks, about 1 to 1½ lbs. total
- 1 envelope onion soup mix

Serves 4

In 12×8-in. dish, combine potatoes, carrots and vegetable beef soup. Cover with plastic wrap. Microwave at High 6 to 8 minutes, or until carrots begin to tenderize, stirring once.

Arrange meat over potatoes and carrots. Sprinkle with onion soup mix. Cover with wax paper. Microwave 5 minutes. Reduce power to 50% (Medium). Microwave 10 to 15 minutes, or until meat is no longer pink, rearranging once.

Microwave	21-28 min.

Cubed Steaks & Brussels ▲ Sprouts Plate

4 cubed steaks
1 envelope onion soup mix
1 pkg. (10 oz.) frozen Brussels sprouts

Serves 4

Coat cubed steaks with onion soup mix. Place in 12×8-in. dish leaving center clear. Arrange frozen Brussels sprouts in center of dish. Cover Brussels sprouts only with plastic wrap. Microwave at High 3 minutes.

Reduce power to 50% (Medium). Microwave 8 minutes. Turn and rearrange steaks. Microwave 8 to 12 minutes, or until meat loses pink color and vegetables are tender-crisp.

NOTE: For softer vegetables, microwave Brussels sprouts at High 1½ minutes before removing from box.

Microwave	19-23 min.

Bacon-Wrapped Mini Meatloaves

½ cup chopped green pepper
½ cup chopped onion
4 thick slices bacon
1 lb. lean ground beef
1 slice bread, moistened with 2 tablespoons milk, torn into pieces
1 egg
2 tablespoons catsup
½ teaspoon salt
⅛ teaspoon pepper
1 tablespoon Worcestershire sauce
1½ teaspoons curry powder
¼ teaspoon bouquet sauce

Serves 4

In small bowl combine green pepper and onion. Cover loosely with plastic wrap. Microwave at High 1 to 1½ minutes, or until tender-crisp. Set aside.

Place bacon on double thickness of paper towels. Cover with paper towel. Microwave at High 2 to 3 minutes, or until slightly underdone.

In medium mixing bowl combine ground beef, green peppers, onion and remaining ingredients. Blend well.

Divide mixture into 2 equal parts, shaping each into a 6×3½-in. loaf. Wrap 2 strips of bacon around each loaf; secure with wooden pick.

Place loaves on roasting rack; cover with wax paper. Microwave at High 7 to 11 minutes, rotating every 2 minutes. Let stand covered 3 minutes, or until firm.

Microwave	10-15½ min.
Standing	3 min.

◂Oriental Meatloaves

4 servings rice
1 lb. lean ground beef
1 can (16 oz.) Chinese vegetables, drained
1 egg
½ cup soy sauce
2 tablespoons sugar
2 teaspoons white cooking wine
½ cup dry bread crumbs

Serves 4 to 6

Cook rice conventionally while microwaving meatloaves.

In medium bowl blend all ingredients thoroughly. Press meatloaf mixture into 4 individual 12-oz. casseroles or 4 cereal bowls. Cover with wax paper. Microwave at High 7 to 8 minutes, rotating 2 or 3 times during cooking. Let stand covered 2 minutes, or until firm to the touch.

To serve, slice thinly and place on a bed of rice.

Microwave	7-8 min.
Standing	2 min.

Individual Mexican Meatloaves

½ cup chopped green pepper
½ cup chopped onion
1 lb. lean ground beef
1 pkg. (1¼ oz.) taco seasoning mix
½ cup chopped tomato
1 egg
½ cup finely crumbled Nacho cheese chips
1 can (15 oz.) kidney beans, drained, optional
4 corn tortillas (6-in.)
¼ cup grated Cheddar cheese, divided
Chopped lettuce
Chopped tomato

Serves 4

In medium mixing bowl combine green pepper and onion. Cover loosely with plastic wrap. Microwave at High 1 to 1½ minutes or until tender-crisp.

Add ground beef, taco seasoning mix, ½ cup chopped tomato, egg, crumbled cheese chips and kidney beans. Set mixture aside.

To fit tortillas in casseroles, cut four 2-in. slashes, 3½ inches apart in edge of each tortilla. Shape tortillas by overlapping cut edges; place in 4 individual 12-oz. casseroles. Press one-fourth of meat mixture into each. Cover with wax paper. Microwave at High 7 to 10 minutes, or until filling is firm to touch.

Top each casserole with 1 tablespoon grated Cheddar cheese. Let stand covered 3 minutes, or until cheese melts. Garnish with chopped lettuce and tomato.

Microwave	8-11½ min.
Standing	3 min.

Saucy Burgers & Rice

1 lb. lean ground beef
½ cup chopped onion, divided
¼ cup soda cracker crumbs
1 egg
1 teaspoon seasoned salt
¼ cup chopped celery
2 cups instant or quick-cooking rice
1 can (4 oz.) mushroom stems and pieces, drained
1 can (10½ oz.) beef broth, divided
⅓ cup water
½ teaspoon bouquet sauce
½ teaspoon water
1 tablespoon and 1 teaspoon cornstarch

Serves 4

Microwave	12½-17½ min.

How to Microwave Saucy Burgers & Rice

Combine ground beef, ¼ cup onion, cracker crumbs, egg and seasoned salt in medium bowl. Shape into 4 oval patties.

Place remaining onion and celery in 2-qt. casserole. Cover. Microwave at High 3 to 4 minutes, or until vegetables are tender.

Stir in rice and mushrooms. Add ⅔ cup beef broth and ⅓ cup water. Arrange patties on top of mixture. Cover.

Microwave at High 7½ to 10½ minutes, or until patties are done and rice is tender, stirring rice and turning outside edge of patties to inside of dish after half the cooking time.

Dilute bouquet sauce with ½ teaspoon water. Brush patties with mixture. Re-cover; let stand while making sauce.

Pour remaining broth into 1-qt. measure. Add water to bring mixture to ¾ cup. Stir in cornstarch. Microwave at High 2 to 3 minutes, or until mixture thickens, stirring twice.

Morning Prayer

Peter Ilyich Tchaikowsky
Op. 39, No. 1

Andante (♩= c. 72)

Bacon Stuffed Patties With Mushrooms & Onions

- 6 slices bacon
- 1 lb. lean ground beef
- 2 tablespoons bread crumbs
- 1 tablespoon parsley flakes
- 1½ teaspoons salt, divided
- ⅛ teaspoon garlic powder
- ⅛ teaspoon pepper
- 8 oz. sliced fresh mushrooms
- 1 medium onion, thinly sliced and separated into rings
- 1 teaspoon Worcestershire sauce

Serves 4

Microwave	15-19 min.

How to Microwave Bacon Stuffed Patties With Mushrooms & Onions

Place bacon on several layers of paper towels. Cover with paper towel. Microwave at High 4 to 6 minutes. Set aside. Preheat browning dish 5 minutes.

Combine ground beef, bread crumbs, parsley flakes, 1 teaspoon salt, garlic powder and pepper. Shape into 8 patties, ¼-in. thick.

Crumble bacon; place one-fourth of bacon on center of each of 4 patties. Top with remaining patties; press edges to seal.

Place patties in preheated browning dish. Microwave at High 1½ minutes. Turn over. Microwave 1½ to 2½ minutes, or until not quite desired doneness.

Remove patties to serving platter. Cover and let stand while preparing vegetables.

Add remaining ingredients to drippings. Microwave at High 2 to 4 minutes, or until vegetables are tender, stirring once. Spoon over patties.

Beef & Beans With Dumplings

1 lb. ground beef
2 envelopes (¾ oz. each) mushroom gravy mix
1½ cups hot water
1 pkg. (9 oz.) frozen cut green beans
1½ cups buttermilk baking mix
1 teaspoon poppy seeds
¼ teaspoon oregano or basil
¼ teaspoon caraway seeds
⅓ cup milk
1 egg
¼ to ⅓ cup seasoned bread crumbs

Serves 4

Microwave	15½-24½ min.

How to Microwave Beef & Beans With Dumplings

Crumble beef into 2-qt. casserole. Microwave at High 3 to 5½ minutes, or until no longer pink, stirring once or twice. Drain fat. Stir in gravy mix and water.

Microwave green beans in package at High 1½ to 2½ minutes, or until package is flexible. Stir beans into meat.

Microwave at High 8 to 11 minutes, or until beans are tender and sauce thickens, stirring once or twice during cooking.

Combine buttermilk baking mix, poppy seeds, oregano and caraway seeds in small mixing bowl, while meat mixture cooks.

Stir milk and egg into dry mixture. Let stand 1 or 2 minutes. Shape into 8 dumplings. Roll each in dry bread crumbs.

Arrange dumplings around top edge of casserole. Microwave at High 3 to 5½ minutes, or until dumplings are firm to touch, rotating dish once or twice.

Meatballs & Baked Beans

- 1 lb. ground beef
- ¼ cup dry bread crumbs
- 1 tablespoon horseradish sauce
- 2 teaspoons Worcestershire sauce, divided
- ½ teaspoon salt
- ⅛ teaspoon garlic powder
- ⅓ cup chopped onion
- ¼ cup chopped celery
- 1 can (28 oz.) baked beans
- ¼ cup catsup
- 1 tablespoon molasses

Serves 4

In medium bowl, combine ground beef, bread crumbs, horseradish, 1 teaspoon Worcestershire sauce, salt and garlic powder. Shape into 18 to 22 meatballs; arrange in 8×8-in. baking dish. Sprinkle with onion and celery.

Microwave at High 5 to 7 minutes, or until meatballs have lost most of their pink color, rearranging and turning over after half the cooking time. Drain.

In medium bowl, combine remaining ingredients. Pour over meatballs. Microwave 5½ to 8 minutes, or until thoroughly heated, stirring gently after half the cooking time.

Microwave 10½-15 min.

Hamburger Stew

- 1½ lbs. lean ground beef
- 1½ cups thinly sliced carrots
- 1 cup thinly sliced celery
- 2 cups hot water
- 1½ cups instant rice
- 1 envelope onion soup mix
- 1 bay leaf

Serves 4 to 6

Crumble beef coarsely into 3 to 5-qt. casserole. Mix in carrots and celery. Cover. Microwave at High 3½ to 6½ minutes, or until beef is set, stirring once or twice.

Add remaining ingredients. Microwave, covered, 12 to 18 minutes, or until vegetables are tender, stirring once or twice. Remove bay leaf before serving.

Microwave 15½-24½ min.

Shepherds Pie

1 lb. ground beef
1 medium onion
1 pkg. (10 oz.) frozen peas and carrots or cut green beans
1 can (10¾ oz.) tomato soup
1 teaspoon Worcestershire sauce
½ teaspoon salt
¼ teaspoon basil
⅛ teaspoon pepper
3 cups hot mashed potatoes, page 132
1 cup shredded Cheddar cheese

Serves 4 to 6

Microwave	13-20 min.
Standing	3 min.

How to Microwave Shepherds Pie

Crumble ground beef into 2-qt. casserole. Add onion. Microwave at High 4 to 6 minutes, or until meat loses its pink color. Break up meat and drain.

Microwave vegetables in package at High 2 to 3½ minutes, or until defrosted.

Chili Rice

1 lb. ground beef
1 medium onion, chopped
½ medium green pepper, chopped
1 clove garlic, minced or pressed
1 can (16 oz.) whole tomatoes, cut up
1 can (15 oz.) kidney beans, drained
1 cup instant rice
1½ teaspoons salt
1 teaspoon sugar
1 teaspoon chili powder
1 cup shredded Cheddar cheese

Serves 4 to 6

Crumble ground beef in 2-qt. casserole. Add onion, green pepper and garlic. Cover. Microwave at High 4 to 6 minutes, or until meat loses most of its pink color and vegetables are tender. Stir to break up meat; drain.

Add remaining ingredients except cheese. Cover. Microwave 16 to 20 minutes, or until rice is tender, stirring after half the time. Sprinkle cheese over top. Cover. Let stand 5 minutes.

Microwave	20-26 min.
Standing	5 min.

Stir tomato soup, Worcestershire sauce, salt, basil and pepper into ground beef mixture while microwaving vegetables. Spread evenly in casserole.

Sprinkle with defrosted vegetables. Spoon mounds of potatoes over vegetables. Microwave 5 to 7 minutes, or until casserole seems hot.

Top with shredded cheese. Microwave 2 to 3½ minutes, or until cheese melts, rotating dish after half the cooking time. Let stand 3 minutes before serving.

Spinach Lasagna

1 pkg. (10 oz.) frozen chopped spinach
1 lb. ground beef
2 tablespoons instant minced onion
⅛ teaspoon garlic powder
1 jar (15½ oz.) spaghetti sauce
¼ cup dry bread crumbs, divided
1 cup creamed cottage cheese
1 egg
⅛ teaspoon pepper
1 cup (4-oz.) shredded mozzarella cheese
2 tablespoons grated Parmesan cheese

Serves 4 to 6

Microwave	19-27 min.
Standing	3 min.

How to Microwave Spinach Lasagna

Microwave spinach in package at High 3 to 4 minutes, or until defrosted. Drain thoroughly and set aside. Crumble ground beef into 2-qt. casserole.

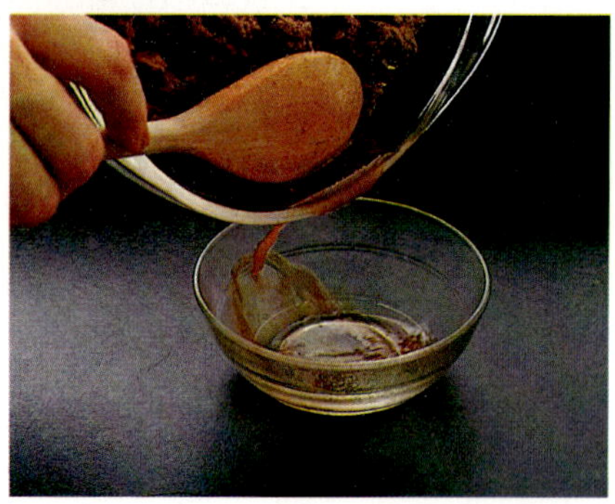

Add minced onion and garlic powder to beef. Microwave at High 4 to 6 minutes,or until meat is no longer pink. Drain.

Stir in spaghetti sauce. Cover. Microwave at High 2 to 4 minutes, or until hot and bubbly, stirring after half the time. Mix in 2 tablespoons bread crumbs.

Combine spinach, cottage cheese, egg, pepper and remaining bread crumbs in medium bowl.

Spread half the meat mixture in 9×9-in. dish. Cover with spinach mixture. Sprinkle with mozzarella. Top with remaining meat; sprinkle with Parmesan.

Microwave at High 3 minutes. Reduce power to 50% (Medium). Microwave 7 to 10 minutes, or until thoroughly heated, rotating dish after half the cooking time. Let stand 3 minutes.

Manicotti

8 manicotti, cooked
½ lb. ground beef
1 tablespoon instant minced onion
⅛ teaspoon garlic powder
1 lb. ricotta cheese
1 cup shredded mozzarella, divided
6 tablespoons grated Parmesan cheese, divided
2 eggs
1 tablespoon parsley flakes
1 teaspoon salt
¼ teaspoon basil
¼ teaspoon oregano
⅛ teaspoon pepper
1 jar (15½ oz.) spaghetti sauce

Serves 4 to 6

Microwave	15-23 min.
Standing	3 min.

How to Microwave Manicotti

Crumble ground beef into 1-qt. casserole; add onion and garlic. Microwave at High 2½ to 4 minutes, or until no longer pink. Break up meat; drain.

Combine in medium bowl ricotta, ½ cup mozzarella, 4 tablespoons Parmesan, eggs, parsley, salt, basil, oregano and pepper. Set aside.

Stir spaghetti sauce into beef. Cover. Microwave at High 1½ to 3 minutes, or until hot, stirring after half the time.

Stuff manicotti with ricotta mixture while microwaving sauce. Spread small amount of sauce in 12×8-in. dish. Place manicotti side by side in dish.

Pour remaining sauce over top. Cover with wax paper. Microwave at High 11 to 16 minutes, or until thoroughly heated, rotating dish after half the cooking time.

Sprinkle remaining ½ cup mozzarella and 2 tablespoons Parmesan over top. Cover. Let stand 3 minutes.

Taco Salad

1 lb. ground beef
1 medium onion, chopped
1 can (15 oz.) kidney beans, drained
½ cup water
½ to 1 pkg. (1¼ oz.) taco seasoning mix
½ medium head lettuce, torn into bite-sized pieces
2 medium tomatoes, cut into chunks
½ medium green pepper, chopped
½ cup shredded Cheddar cheese
½ cup shredded Monterey Jack cheese
1 cup broken corn chips

Serves 4 to 6

Microwave	14½-19½ min.

How to Microwave Taco Salad

Crumble ground beef into 2-qt. casserole; add onion. Microwave at High 4½ to 6½ minutes, or until meat loses its pink color, stirring to break up meat after half the cooking time. Drain.

Stir in beans, water and taco seasoning. Microwave uncovered at 50% (Medium) 10 to 13 minutes, or until thick and bubbly, stirring once.

Combine lettuce, tomatoes and green pepper in salad bowl while meat and beans cook. Spoon mixture over lettuce. Top with cheeses, then corn chips. Serve immediately with chili sauce or taco sauce.

Hamburger Quiche

½ lb. ground beef
4 eggs
½ cup sliced green onion
⅓ cup milk
⅓ cup mayonnaise
½ teaspoon salt
⅛ teaspoon pepper
¾ cup shredded Cheddar cheese

Serves 4

Crumble ground beef into 9-in. pie plate. Microwave at High 2½ to 4 minutes, or until meat loses its pink color. Break up and drain.

In medium bowl, combine remaining ingredients except cheese. Pour into pie plate.

Reduce power to 50% (Medium). Microwave 4 minutes. Push cooked portions to center of plate. Microwave 4½ to 8 minutes, or until almost set, lifting edges of set egg after half the cooking time. Sprinkle with cheese. Microwave 1 to 2½ minutes, or until cheese melts. Let stand several minutes before serving.

Microwave	12-18½ min.
Standing	2-3 min.

Veal Parmigiana

- 1 tablespoon olive oil
- 1/4 cup chopped onion
- 1 can (8 oz.) tomato sauce
- 1/2 teaspoon basil leaves
- 3/4 to 1 lb. veal cutlets, flattened to 1/8-in. thickness
- 1 egg, beaten
- 1/3 cup finely crushed corn flake crumbs
- 3/4 cup shredded mozzarella
- 1 tablespoon Parmesan cheese

Serves 2 to 4

In 4-cup measure, combine oil and onions. Microwave at High 1 to 2 minutes, or until onion is tender. Stir in tomato sauce and basil. Microwave at High 3 to 5 minutes, or until sauce is hot and somewhat thickened.

Dip veal pieces in egg; dredge in crumbs. Place in 12×8-in. dish. Cover with wax paper. Microwave at High 3½ to 5 minutes, or until veal is fork tender.

Pour sauce over veal, sprinkle with mozzarella, top with Parmesan. Microwave, uncovered, at 50% (Medium) 2 to 3 minutes, or until cheese melts.

Microwave 9½-15 min.

Lemon-Dill Veal ▲

½ cup dry seasoned bread crumbs
¾ teaspoon dill weed
1 egg, beaten
2 teaspoons lemon juice
4 veal cube steaks (about 1 lb.)
2 tablespoons butter or margarine
1 cup sliced fresh mushrooms
¼ cup chopped onions

Serves 4

On waxed paper, combine bread crumbs and dill weed. Set aside. Blend egg and lemon juice in shallow bowl. Dip steaks into egg mixture and dredge in bread crumbs.

Preheat 10-in. browning dish at High 5 minutes. Quickly add butter and veal. Microwave at High 45 seconds. Turn. Add mushrooms and onions. Cover. Microwave at High 4 to 6 minutes or until veal and vegetables are fork tender, rearranging steaks after 2 minutes.

Microwave	9¾-11¾ min.

Veal in Sour Cream ▸

1 tablespoon butter or margarine
1 lb. veal cube steaks or cutlets
8 oz. fresh mushrooms, sliced
1 tablespoon grated onion
1 cup (8 oz.) sour cream
¼ cup sherry
1 teaspoon salt*
2 tablespoons flour

Serves 4

Preheat 10-in. browning dish at High 5 minutes. Add butter and veal. Let veal stand 15 to 20 seconds. Turn cutlets over. Add mushrooms and onion. Microwave at High 1 to 2 minutes, or until mushrooms are tender, rotating cutlets after half the cooking time.

In 2-cup measure, mix sour cream, sherry and salt. Blend in flour. Stir sour cream mixture into veal and mushrooms. Microwave at 50% (Medium) 1 to 2 minutes, or until sauce is hot and slightly thickened.

*Omit salt if using cooking sherry.

Microwave	7-9 min.
Standing	15-20 sec.

Pork Schnitzel

1½ to 1¾ lbs. pork chops or steaks
3 tablespoons flour
½ teaspoon salt
⅛ teaspoon pepper
⅛ teaspoon ground cloves, optional
1 egg
2 tablespoons milk
⅔ cup dry bread crumbs
2 teaspoons parsley flakes
½ teaspoon paprika
1½ tablespoon oil

Serves 4

Microwave	10½-14 min.

How to Microwave Pork Schnitzel

Remove bone and trim fat from chops or steaks. Pound to ¼-in. thickness with the edge of a saucer or a meat mallet.

Combine flour, salt, pepper and cloves on wax paper.

Blend egg and milk in small bowl. On another sheet of wax paper combine bread crumbs, parsley flakes and paprika.

Dredge chops or steaks lightly in seasoned flour. Dip in egg, then coat with crumbs. Set aside.

Preheat browning dish at High 5 minutes. Add oil; tilt dish to coat bottom. Place chops in dish.

Microwave at High 2 minutes. Turn chops over; microwave 3½ to 7 minutes, or until meat is no longer pink.

Barbecue Pork Chops ▲

½ cup chopped onion
4 pork chops, ½-in. thick
⅔ cup catsup
¼ cup brown sugar
1 tablespoon lemon juice
¼ teaspoon dry mustard
⅛ teaspoon allspice
⅛ teaspoon pepper

Serves 4

Place chopped onion in 12×8-in. glass baking dish. Microwave at High 1½ to 2½ minutes, or until tender. Arrange chops over onion with meatiest portions to outside of dish.

Combine remaining ingredients in small bowl. Spoon half the mixture over chops. Microwave at High 3 minutes. Reduce power to 50% (Medium). Microwave for 7 minutes.

Turn over and rearrange chops. Spoon remaining sauce over top. Microwave at 50% (Medium) 7 to 12 minutes, or until meat next to bone is no longer pink.

Microwave	18½-24½ min.

Gingered Ham Kabobs ►

1 large green pepper, cut into 16 cubes (1½-in.)
1½ lbs. fully cooked ham, cut into 32 cubes (1-in.)
1 can (5¼ oz.) chunk pineapple, ¼ cup juice reserved
1 can (23 oz.) sweet potatoes, cut into 16 chunks (1½-in.)
1 jar (16 oz.) spiced whole crab apples

Glaze:

¼ cup pineapple juice
2 teaspoons lemon juice
¼ cup honey
¼ cup brown sugar
1 teaspoon ground ginger

Serves 4

Place green pepper in small bowl. Cover with plastic wrap. Microwave at High 1 to 2 minutes, or until tender-crisp.

In a 2-cup measure combine glaze ingredients. Microwave at High 1 to 1½ minutes, or until mixture boils. Set aside.

Arrange kabobs on 8 skewers as shown at right. Place on roasting rack or baking sheet. Baste with half of glaze. Cover with wax paper. Microwave at High 6 to 7 minutes, or until hot, rotating after half the time. Serve with remaining glaze.

Microwave	8-10½ min.

Glazed Ham & Sweet Potatoes

1 can (23 oz.) sweet potatoes (or yams) in syrup, drained and cut in 1-in. cubes
1 to 1¼ lb. fully cooked, boneless ham slices, ½-in. thick
¼ cup maple syrup
¼ cup brown sugar
¼ teaspoon dry mustard
Dash cloves

Serves 4

Arrange sweet potatoes around edges of 12×8-in. dish. Place ham slices in center, overlapping slightly to fit dish.

Combine remaining ingredients to make glaze; pour half over ham and sweet potatoes. Cover dish with wax paper. Microwave at High 4 minutes.

Pour remaining glaze over ham and sweet potatoes. Do not cover. Microwave at High 4 to 7 minutes or until ham is hot.

Microwave 8-11 min.

Ham & Zucchini in Cheese Sauce

4 servings rice or noodles
4 cups thinly sliced zucchini
¼ cup chopped onion
2 tablespoons water
2 tablespoons butter or margarine
2 tablespoons flour
½ teaspoon salt
⅛ teaspoon pepper
¾ cup milk
½ cup shredded Cheddar cheese
2 cups cubed cooked ham
¼ teaspoon paprika

Serves 4

Cook rice or noodles conventionally while microwaving sauce. Combine zucchini, onion and water in 2-qt. casserole. Cover. Microwave at High 4 to 7 minutes, or until zucchini is tender-crisp. Let stand covered while making sauce.

Melt butter in 4-cup measure at High 30 to 60 seconds. Stir in flour, salt and pepper until smooth. Blend in milk. Microwave at High 4 to 6 minutes, or until thickened, stirring every minute. Stir in cheese.

Drain zucchini. Add ham and cheese sauce to zucchini. Microwave at High 2 to 3½ minutes, or until thoroughly heated.

Stir mixture to redistribute sauce. Sprinkle paprika on top. Serve over rice or noodles.

Microwave 10½-17½ min.

Ham & Cheese Filled Cabbage Rolls

6 large cabbage leaves

Filling:
2 cups cooked cubed ham
1 cup shredded Cheddar cheese
1 egg
¼ cup seasoned bread crumbs
¼ teaspoon dry mustard

Topping:
3 tablespoons grated Parmesan cheese
2 tablespoons shredded Cheddar cheese
¼ teaspoon paprika

Note: To remove cabbage leaves, microwave the whole cabbage head at High 1 to 3 minutes,or until 6 outer leaves can be separated easily. Refrigerate remaining cabbage for future use.

Serves 6

Microwave 7½-14 min.

How to Microwave Ham & Cheese Filled Cabbage Rolls

Cut out hard center rib from each cabbage leaf. Place leaves in 8×8-in. dish. Cover with vented plastic wrap. Microwave at High 1 to 2½ minutes, or until leaves are pliable. Set aside.

Combine filling ingredients. Place one-sixth of the mixture on the base of each leaf. Fold in sides of leaf. Roll up leaves to enclose filling. Secure with a pick if necessary. Place rolls, seam side down, in 8×8-in. dish. Cover with wax paper.

Microwave 4 to 6 minutes, or until filling is set, rotating dish after half the cooking time. Combine topping ingredients. Sprinkle over rolls. Microwave uncovered 1½ to 2½ minutes, or until cheese melts.

Lamb Meatballs With Dill Sauce

4 servings noodles

Meatballs:
- 1 lb. ground lamb
- ⅓ cup quick-cooking oats
- 1 egg
- ¼ cup chopped onion
- 1 teaspoon salt
- ⅛ teaspoon pepper

Sauce:
- 2 tablespoons butter or margarine
- 2 tablespoons flour
- ½ teaspoon dill weed
- ½ teaspoon paprika, divided
- ¼ teaspoon salt
- ⅛ teaspoon pepper
- 1 cup milk

Serves 4

Cook noodles conventionally while microwaving meatballs. In medium bowl combine meatball ingredients. Shape into 15 to 18 meatballs. Place in 12×8-in. baking dish. Microwave at High 6 to 8 minutes, or until no longer pink, turning over and rearranging after half the cooking time. Drain; remove to serving platter, if desired. Cover to keep warm.

In 1-qt. measure melt butter at High 30 to 40 seconds. Stir in flour, dill weed, ¼ teaspoon paprika, salt and pepper. Blend in milk. Microwave at High 4 to 5 minutes, or until thickened, stirring every minute.

Pour sauce over meatballs. Sprinkle evenly with remaining paprika. Microwave at High 1 minute to reheat.

Serve with hot buttered noodles.

Microwave	11½-14¾ min.

Lamb Burgers

4 slices bacon
1 lb. ground lamb
⅓ cup chopped green onion
1½ teaspoons Worcestershire sauce
½ teaspoon seasoned salt
4 slices Monterey Jack cheese

Serves 4

Place bacon on two layers of paper towels. Cover with paper towel. Microwave at High 3 to 4 minutes, or until slightly underdone. Set aside. Preheat browning grill at High 5 minutes.

While microwaving bacon and preheating grill, prepare lamb burgers. In medium bowl combine lamb, green onion, Worcestershire sauce and salt. Shape into 4 patties.

Place patties in preheated dish. Microwave at High 2 minutes. Turn over. Microwave at High 2 to 3 minutes, or until patties are desired doneness.

Cut bacon slices in half. Place two halves on each patty. Top each with a cheese slice. Cover dish. Microwave at High 1 minute to melt cheese.

Serve on buns or hard rolls.

Microwave	13-15 min.

Lamb Creole

1 medium onion, chopped
1 stalk celery, chopped
½ medium green pepper, chopped
1 tablespoon olive oil
1½ cups cooked lamb, cut into ¾-in. cubes
1½ cups quick-cooking rice
1 can (8 oz.) tomato sauce
¾ cup water
1 can (4 oz.) mushroom stems and pieces, drained
2 teaspoons brown sugar
½ teaspoon basil
½ teaspoon salt
⅛ teaspoon pepper
1 bay leaf
⅛ teaspoon thyme
⅛ teaspoon red pepper

Serves 4

In 2-qt. casserole combine onion, celery, green pepper and oil. Cover; microwave at High 3 to 5 minutes, or until tender.

Stir in remaining ingredients. Cover. Microwave at High 5 minutes. Stir; re-cover.

Reduce power to 50% (Medium). Microwave 5 to 8 minutes, or until rice is tender and all liquid is absorbed, stirring once during cooking.

Microwave	13-18 min.

◂ Polynesian Bean & Wiener Bake

1 medium apple, chopped
½ cup chopped onion
1 tablespoon butter or margarine
1 tablespoon cornstarch
2 cans (16 oz.) kidney beans, drained
1 can (16 oz.) baked beans
½ lb. wieners, cut into ½-in. pieces
2 tablespoons molasses
2 tablespoons vinegar
½ teaspoon dry mustard
¼ teaspoon salt
⅛ teaspoon pepper
1 can (8¼ oz.) pineapple chunks, drained

Serves 4 to 6

In 2-qt. casserole combine apple, onion, butter and cornstarch. Microwave at High 2½ to 3 minutes or until tender.

Add remaining ingredients. Microwave at High 8 to 10 minutes, or until sauce is thickened and casserole is heated through, stirring once or twice during cooking.

Microwave	10½-13 min.

Polish Sausages & Creamy Potatoes ▸

4 medium potatoes, peeled and sliced ¼-in. thick
¼ cup water
½ teaspoon salt
1 pkg. (3 oz.) cream cheese
½ cup milk
1 tablespoon flour
2 teaspoons chives
½ teaspoon dry mustard
⅛ teaspoon pepper
½ teaspoon caraway seed
6 fully cooked Polish sausages, slit diagonally at 1-in. intervals

Serves 4

In 2-qt. casserole combine sliced potatoes and water. Cover. Microwave at High 6 to 8 minutes, or until potatoes are fork tender, stirring after half the cooking time. Drain; sprinkle with salt. Set aside.

Soften cream cheese in 2-cup measure or small bowl at High 15 to 30 seconds. Stir in milk, flour and seasonings. Microwave at High 1 to 2 minutes, or until thickened, stirring once or twice.

Blend cream cheese mixture into potatoes. Arrange Polish sausages on top of potatoes, around outer edges of casserole. Cover. Microwave at High 4½ minutes, or until sausages are heated through, rotating dish ½ turn after half the cooking time.

Microwave	11¾-15 min.

Link Sausage & Cheesy Potatoes

1 pkg. (12 oz.) frozen shredded hash brown potatoes
1½ cups shredded Cheddar or American cheese
⅓ cup milk
2 teaspoons chopped chives
½ teaspoon salt
¼ teaspoon dry mustard
Dash pepper
1 pkg. (8 oz.) frozen fully cooked pork sausage links
½ teaspoon bouquet sauce
½ teaspoon water

Serves 4

Variation:
1 pkg. (12 oz.) frozen uncooked sausage links

Before defrosting potatoes, place links on baking rack; cover with wax paper. Microwave at High 4 to 6 minutes, or until almost cooked. Combine bouquet sauce and water. Turn links over, rearrange and brush with bouquet mixture after half the cooking time. Set aside. Place links on top of potatoes after first 6 minutes of cooking.

Microwave 13½-17 min.

How to Microwave Link Sausage & Cheesy Potatoes

Place hash browns in 8×8-in. dish. Cover with wax paper. Microwave at High 5 to 7 minutes, or until potatoes are defrosted, breaking into small pieces after 4 minutes.

Stir in cheese, milk and seasonings. Spread evenly in dish. Arrange frozen sausage links on top. Re-cover. Microwave at High 6 minutes.

Remove sausages and stir potatoes. Arrange sausages on top. Combine bouquet sauce and water. Brush tops of sausages with bouquet mixture.

Microwave at High uncovered 2½ to 4 minutes, or until sausages are hot and potatoes are tender.

Company Macaroni, Sausage & Cheese

- 1 pkg. (7 oz.) elbow macaroni
- 4 tablespoons butter or margarine, divided
- 1½ tablespoons cornstarch
- 1 teaspoon salt
- 1 teaspoon prepared mustard
- ¼ teaspoon pepper
- 1½ cups milk
- 1½ cups grated Cheddar or American cheese
- 1 pkg. (8 oz.) brown and serve sausages, cut into ½-in. pieces
- ½ cup chopped green onion, tops included
- 3 tablespoons dry bread
- ½ teaspoon parsley flakes

Serves 4 to 6

Cook macaroni conventionally for minimum time while microwaving sauce. Melt 3 tablespoons butter in 2-qt. casserole at High 30 to 45 seconds. Stir in cornstarch. Add salt, mustard and pepper. Blend in milk. Microwave at High 6 to 7 minutes, or until thickened, stirring after the first 2 minutes, then every minute. Stir in cheese until melted; microwave 15 seconds if needed.

Mix in macaroni, sausage and onion. Set aside. Place remaining butter in small dish. Microwave at High 15 to 30 seconds, or until melted. Stir in bread crumbs and parsley flakes. Set aside.

Microwave macaroni mixture at High 3 minutes. Stir. Sprinkle bread crumb mixture over top. Microwave 2 to 3 minutes longer, or until thoroughly heated.

Microwave	12-14½ min.

Open Face Cheese Dogs

2 slices bread, toasted and cut in half
Mayonnaise, optional
Mustard, optional
Relish, optional
4 hot dogs, split lengthwise
4 slices Cheddar or American cheese, cut in half

Serves 2 to 4

Line bottom of 12×8-in. dish with paper towel. Arrange toast halves in dish. Spread lightly with mayonnaise, mustard and/or relish, if desired. Top each toast half with a hot dog and half slice cheese.

Microwave at High 2 to 2½ minutes, or until hot dogs are heated through and cheese is softened, rotating dish ½ turn after half the cooking time.

Microwave 2-2½ min.

Wieners & Sauerkraut

1 medium apple, chopped
½ cup chopped onion
¼ cup chopped celery
1 can (16 oz.) sauerkraut, well drained
1 can (8 oz.) crushed pineapple, well drained
2 teaspoons sugar
1 teaspoon cornstarch
1 teaspoon salt
⅛ teaspoon garlic powder
⅛ teaspoon pepper
8 wieners, cut in fourths

Serves 4

Combine apple, onion and celery in 2-qt. casserole. Cover. Microwave at High 3 to 5 minutes, or until celery is tender.

Stir in remaining ingredients except wieners. Add wieners and push to bottom of casserole so they are covered with the sauerkraut mixture. Cover. Microwave 6 to 9 minutes, or until thoroughly heated, stirring after half the cooking time.

Microwave 9-14 min.

Texas Cornbread Casserole

½ lb. ground sausage
½ lb. ground beef
1 medium onion, chopped
½ medium green pepper, chopped
1 can (10¾ oz.) tomato soup
1 tablespoon brown sugar
2 teaspoons vinegar
1 teaspoon Worcestershire sauce
¼ teaspoon salt
¼ teaspoon garlic powder
⅛ teaspoon pepper
1 teaspoon chili powder
1 pkg. (8½ oz.) cornbread mix
⅛ teaspoon paprika

Serves 4

In 8×8-in. baking dish combine sausage, ground beef, onion and green pepper. Cover with wax paper. Microwave at High 3 to 5 minutes, or until meat is no longer pink, stirring to break up meat after half of the cooking time. Stir; drain.

Mix in remaining ingredients except cornbread mix and paprika. Microwave at High 3 to 4 minutes, or until bubbly. Stir. While meat is microwaving, prepare cornbread as directed on package. Spread on hot meat mixture. Sprinkle evenly with paprika. Microwave at High 6 to 7 minutes, or until cornbread is set, rotating dish ½ turn after half the cooking time. Let stand 2 to 3 minutes.

Microwave	12-16 min.
Standing	2-3 min.

Bologna Kabobs

1½ tablespoons brown sugar
1 teaspoon cornstarch
2 teaspoons soy sauce
1 can (8 oz.) pineapple chunks, drained and juice reserved
1 ring (1 lb.) bologna, skinned and cut into 16 chunks
½ medium green pepper, cut into 12 pieces (¾-in.)

Serves 2 to 4

In 1-cup measure combine brown sugar and cornstarch. Add soy sauce and pineapple juice. Microwave at High 1 to 1¾ minutes, or until thickened, stirring after half the cooking time.

While sauce is cooking, assemble kabobs. Score ends of each bologna chunk with fork tine. On each skewer place 1 bologna chunk, green pepper piece, 2 pineapple chunks, green pepper piece, bologna chunk. Repeat sequence once, separating the two sequences with 1 pineapple chunk.

Place kabobs on roasting rack. Brush kabobs with half of pineapple glaze. Cover with wax paper. Microwave at High 3 minutes. Turn over and rearrange kabobs.

Brush with remaining glaze; recover. Microwave at High 2 to 3 minutes, or until bologna chunks are thoroughly heated; green pepper will be tender-crisp.

Microwave	6-7¾ min.

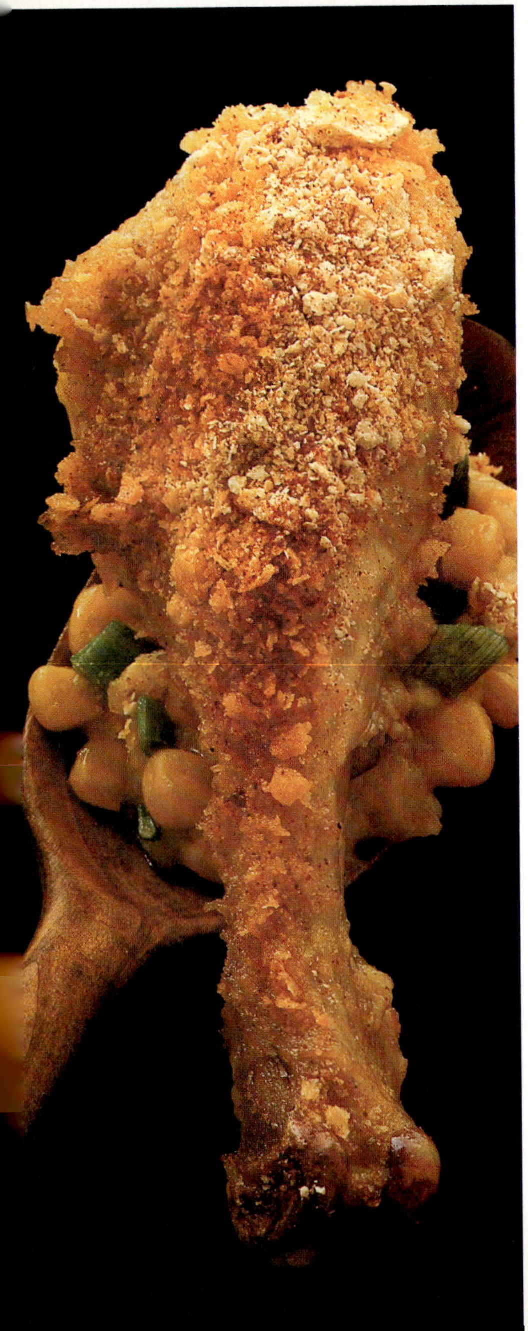

◂Chicken on Scalloped Corn

- 1 can (16 oz.) cream-style corn
- 1 cup saltine cracker crumbs, divided
- ½ cup milk
- ½ cup chopped green onion
- 1 egg
- 1 tablespoon flour
- 2½ to 3 lbs. broiler-fryer chicken pieces, skin removed if desired
- ¼ teaspoon paprika

Serves 4

In 12×8-in. baking dish combine corn, ¾ cup cracker crumbs, milk, onion, egg and flour. Arrange chicken pieces on top, bony side up. Microwave at High 10 minutes.

Stir corn mixture well. Turn over and rearrange chicken pieces, placing least done parts to outside of dish. Combine remaining cracker crumbs and paprika in small bowl. Sprinkle over chicken.

Microwave 10 to 15 minutes, or until chicken is done and corn is set. Excess fat may be drained.

Microwave 20-25 min.

Chicken & Rice▴

- 1 medium onion, chopped
- 1 cup chopped green pepper
- 1 tablespoon olive oil
- 2 cups quick-cooking rice
- 1¾ cups tomato juice
- 1 cup frozen peas
- ⅓ cup chopped stuffed olives
- 1 teaspoon sugar
- ½ teaspoon salt
- ⅛ teaspoon pepper
- 5 to 6 drops red hot sauce
- 2 to 2½ lbs. broiler-fryer chicken pieces, skin removed if desired
- ¼ teaspoon paprika

Serves 4

In 12×8-in. dish combine onion, green pepper and olive oil. Microwave at High 3½ minutes, or until tender.

Stir in all ingredients except chicken and paprika. Arrange chicken on top, bony side up and meatiest portions to outer edges of dish. Cover with plastic wrap.

Microwave at High 10 minutes; turn over and rearrange chicken; rotate dish. Sprinkle with paprika. Re-cover.

Microwave at High 7 to 10 minutes, or until meat is no longer pink and rice is tender.

Microwave 20½-23½ min.

Cranberry-Orange Chicken

1 can (16 oz.) whole cranberry sauce
1 tablespoon brown sugar
1 tablespoon orange juice concentrate, thawed
1 teaspoon bouquet sauce
1 tablespoon water
3 lbs. broiler-fryer chicken pieces, skin removed if desired

Serves 4

Microwave 18-22 min.

How to Microwave Cranberry-Orange Chicken

Combine cranberry sauce, brown sugar, and orange juice in medium bowl. Set aside. Combine bouquet sauce and water.

Arrange chicken pieces bony side up on roasting rack. Brush with half bouquet sauce. Cover with wax paper. Microwave at High 10 minutes. Drain.

Brush lightly with cranberry sauce. Turn chicken pieces over. Brush with remaining bouquet sauce; re-cover. Microwave at High 5 minutes. Remove wax paper.

Brush again with cranberry sauce. Microwave uncovered at High 3 to 7 minutes, or until meat loses its pink color. If desired, reheat remaining sauce and garnish with orange slices.

Chicken in Creamy Tomato Sauce

4 servings noodles or rice
¼ cup chopped onion
1 tablespoon butter or margarine
1 can (8 oz.) tomato sauce
1 tablespoon cornstarch
1 teaspoon sugar
½ teaspoon salt
¼ teaspoon basil
¼ teaspoon marjoram
⅛ teaspoon garlic powder
⅛ teaspoon pepper
¼ cup white wine or ¼ cup water plus 2 teaspoons instant chicken bouillon
2 to 3 lbs. broiler-fryer chicken pieces, skin removed if desired
½ cup whipping cream or sour cream
2 tablespoons grated Parmesan cheese
¼ cup slivered almonds

Serves 4

Microwave	19-24 min.

How to Microwave Chicken in Creamy Tomato Sauce

Cook noodles or rice conventionally. Combine onion and butter in shallow 3 to 5-qt. casserole. Cover. Microwave at High 2 to 3 minutes or until tender. Stir in tomato sauce, cornstarch, sugar and seasonings. Add wine.

Place chicken pieces in casserole and spoon sauce over to coat. Cover. Microwave at High 17 to 21 minutes, or until meat is no longer pink, stirring twice during cooking.

Remove chicken pieces to serving platter. Skim fat if skin wasn't removed. Stir cream and cheese into sauce. Pour sauce over chicken. Sprinkle with almonds and additional Parmesan cheese, if desired. Serve with noodles or rice.

Orange-Walnut Chicken

- 4 servings rice
- 6 oz. frozen concentrated orange juice, thawed
- ¾ cup water, divided
- 1 teaspoon poultry seasoning
- 1 teaspoon salt
- 3 to 4 lbs. broiler-fryer chicken pieces, skin removed if desired
- 2 tablespoons cornstarch
- ¼ cup chopped green onions
- ½ cup walnut halves

Serves 4

Cook rice conventionally while microwaving chicken. Combine orange juice, ½ cup water, poultry seasoning and salt in 2-cup measure. Arrange chicken in 12×8-in. baking dish with meatiest portions to the outside. Pour orange sauce over chicken; cover with wax paper. Microwave at High 15 to 20 minutes or until chicken is tender, turning less cooked portions to outside after half the cooking time. Combine ¼ cup water and cornstarch in 1-cup measure.

Remove chicken to serving platter. Skim fat, if needed. Gradually stir cornstarch mixture, green onions and walnuts into sauce.

Microwave at High 2 minutes, or until thickened, stirring after 1 minute. Pour sauce over chicken. Serve with rice.

Microwave	17-22 min.

Souper Chicken

- 6 tablespoons flour, divided
- 1 envelope (2 oz.) dry chicken noodle soup mix, divided
- 2 teaspoons parsley flakes
- ¼ teaspoon paprika
- 2½ to 3 lbs. broiler-fryer chicken pieces, skin removed if desired
- 1½ cups water

Serves 4

Combine 4 tablespoons flour, ½ envelope soup mix, parsley flakes and paprika. Coat chicken pieces with the mixture. Sprinkle any remaining mixture over pieces.

In 12×8-in. dish mix remaining flour, soup mix and water. Arrange chicken pieces in dish. Cover with wax paper. Microwave at High 20 to 25 minutes, or until chicken is no longer pink, rearranging but not turning over pieces and stirring gravy after half the time.

Microwave	20-25 min.

Chicken & Spinach Stir-Fry

4 servings rice or chow mein noodles
1 pkg. (6 oz.) frozen pea pods
¼ cup soy sauce
1 tablespoon sherry
1 tablespoon cornstarch
1 teaspoon sugar
¼ teaspoon salt
⅛ teaspoon nutmeg
¼ teaspoon ginger
⅛ teaspoon garlic powder
¾ to 1 lb. boneless chicken breasts, cut into strips
2 tablespoons butter or margarine
1 cup thinly sliced celery
8 oz. fresh spinach, washed, stems removed and torn in bite-size pieces
⅓ cup slivered almonds

Serves 2 to 4

Microwave 11½-14½ min.

How to Microwave Chicken & Spinach Stir-Fry

Cook rice conventionally, or microwave following directions on page 132. Microwave pea pods in package at High 1½ to 2½ minutes, or until defrosted.

Combine soy sauce, sherry, cornstarch, sugar, salt, nutmeg, ginger and garlic in small bowl. Stir in chicken; set aside.

Preheat 10-in. browning dish at High 5 minutes while preparing celery and spinach. Add butter to dish; swirl to coat.

Add chicken and marinade; stir immediately to prevent sticking. Microwave at High 2 minutes, stirring after 1 minute.

Stir in celery. Cover; microwave at High 1 minute. Mix in spinach and pea pods. Cover.

Microwave at High 2 to 4 minutes, or until vegetables are tender, stirring once during cooking. Stir in almonds. Serve with rice or chow mein noodles.

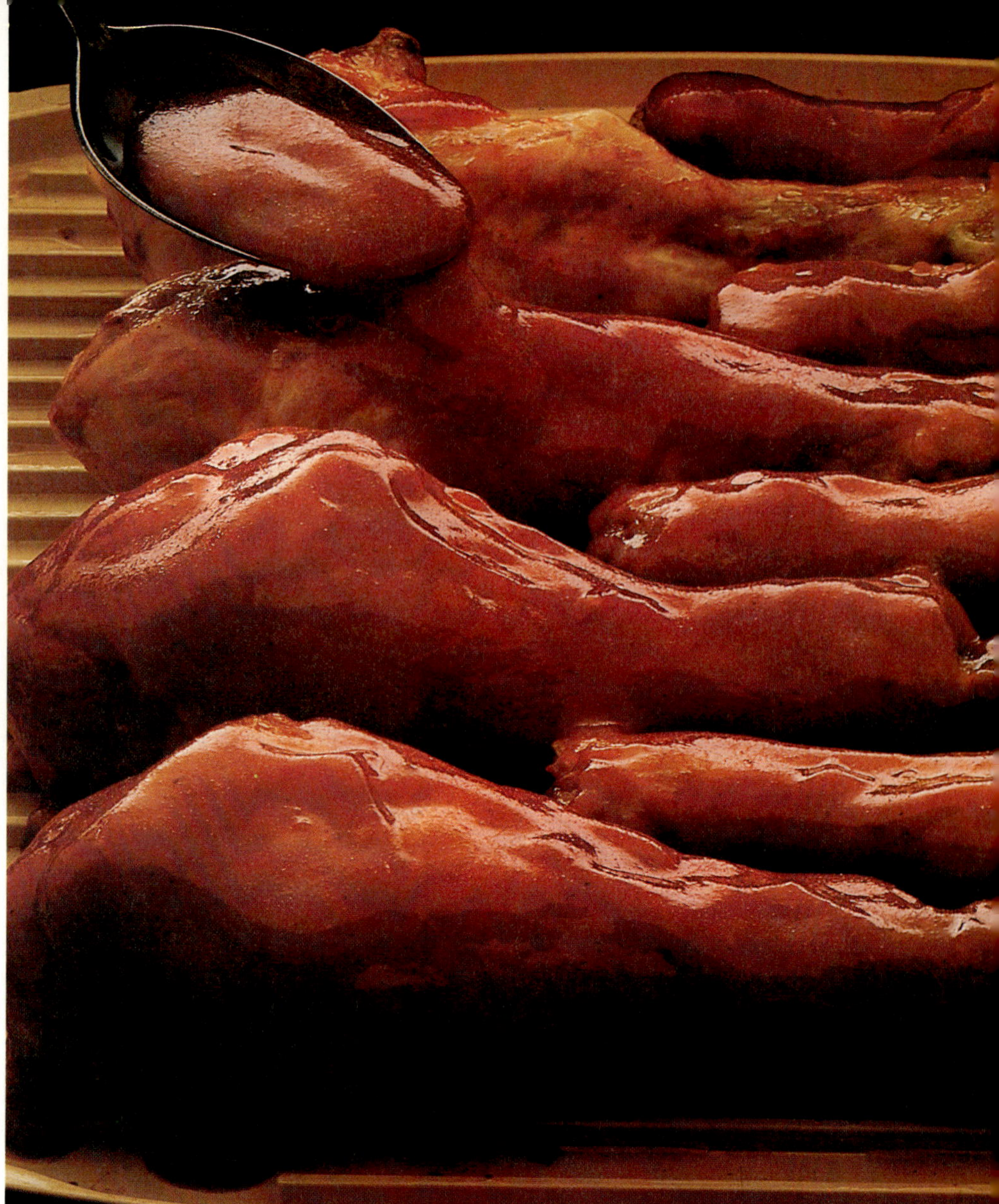

Smoky Barbecued Drumsticks

2 tablespoons butter or margarine
⅔ cup catsup
⅓ cup brown sugar
2 teaspoons lemon juice
1 teaspoon liquid smoke
⅛ teaspoon nutmeg
⅛ teaspoon allspice
⅛ teaspoon garlic powder
8 chicken drumsticks, skin removed if desired

Serves 4

Variation:
Apricot-Sauced Drumsticks: Combine 1 jar (12 oz.) apricot preserves and 1 teaspoon lemon juice in 2-cup measure. Microwave at High 1 to 1½ minutes. Spoon on drumsticks as directed.

Microwave	12½-15 min.

How to Microwave Smoky Barbecued Drumsticks

Melt butter in 2-cup measure at High 30 to 60 seconds. Stir in remaining ingredients except drumsticks.

Arrange drumsticks on roasting rack, meatiest portions to outside of dish. Spoon one-third of sauce over drumsticks. Cover with wax paper. Microwave at High 6 minutes.

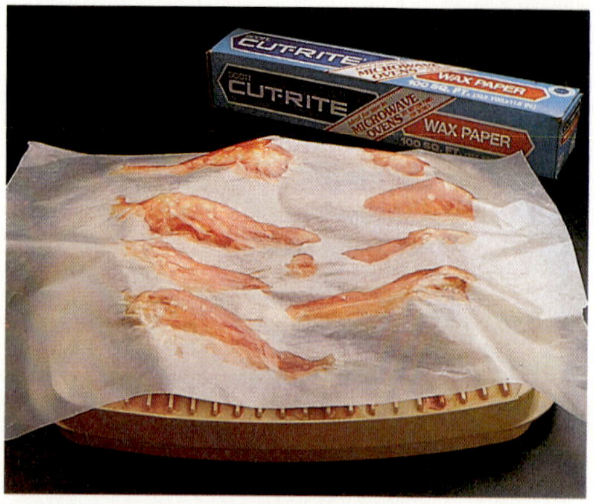

Turn over drumsticks; spoon on another one-third of sauce. Cover with wax paper. Microwave at High 5 to 6 minutes, or until meat is no longer pink. Drain.

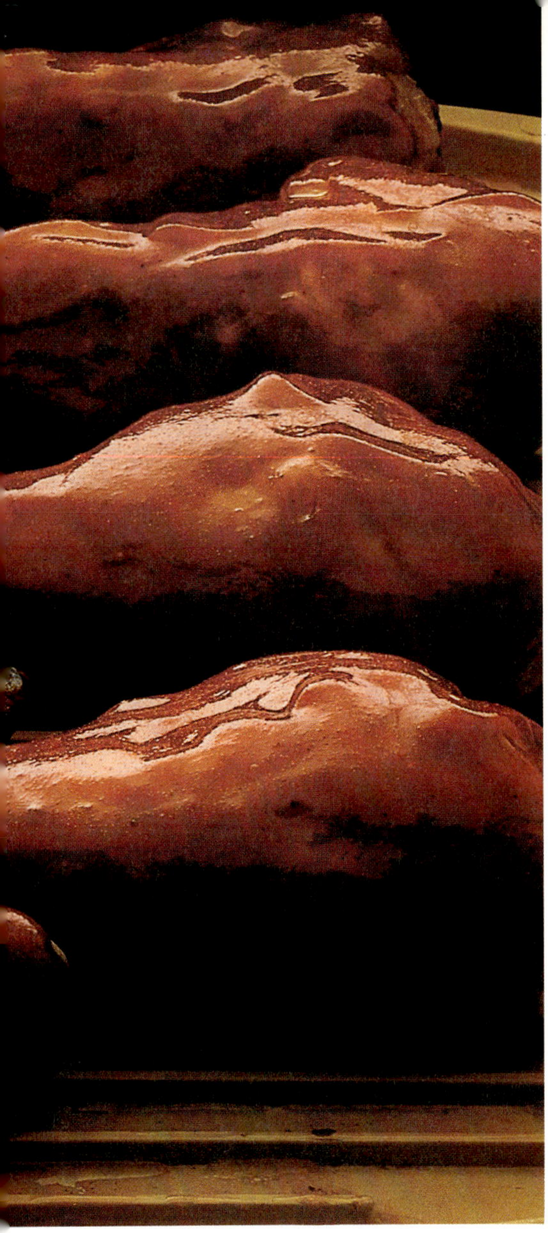

Spoon remaining sauce over drumsticks. Microwave uncovered at High 1 to 2 minutes to heat sauce.

Chicken With French Green Beans Dinner

- ⅓ cup dry seasoned bread crumbs
- 3 tablespoons soy sauce, divided
- 2 pkgs. (10 oz. each) frozen French style green beans
- ¾ cup sliced almonds
- 2 whole bone-in chicken breasts, skinned and halved

Serves 4

In a small bowl combine bread crumbs and 2 tablespoons soy sauce. Stir to coat crumbs evenly.

Microwave green beans in their packages at High 2 to 3 minutes, or until package is flexible. Drain any excess water. Combine beans, almonds and remaining soy sauce in 12×8-in. dish.

Coat chicken with bread crumbs, pressing lightly so crumbs will adhere. Arrange over bean mixture wih meatiest portion to outside of dish. Microwave at High 8 minutes. Rearrange chicken. Microwave 8 to 12 minutes, or until meat near bone is no longer pink.

Microwave 18-23 min.

Company Chicken Breasts ▸

- 4 servings rice or noodles
- 2 oz. chipped beef
- 2 whole boneless chicken breasts, skinned and halved, flattened to ¼-in. thick
- 16 oz. fresh mushrooms, thinly sliced
- 1 can (10¾ oz.) cream of mushroom soup
- ½ cup sour cream
- ¼ cup sliced almonds

Serves 4

Cook rice or noodles conventionally while microwaving chicken. Place one-fourth of chipped beef on each half breast. Roll up breasts and secure with wooden picks.

Place sliced mushrooms in 8×8-in. dish. Arrange rolled breasts on top. Combine soup and sour cream; spoon over chicken. Cover with wax paper. Microwave at High 7½ to 12½ minutes, or until chicken is no longer pink, rearranging after half the cooking time.

Sprinkle almonds over chicken. Serve with rice or noodles.

Microwave	7½-12½ min.

Chicken Breasts With Wine & Mushrooms

- 2 whole boneless chicken breasts, skinned and halved
- 8 oz. fresh mushrooms, sliced
- ¼ cup butter
- 3 tablespoons flour
- ½ teaspoon salt
- ⅛ teaspoon pepper
- ⅓ cup heavy cream
- ¼ cup dry sherry
- 1 egg yolk, beaten
- 1 teaspoon parsley flakes
- 2 to 3 drops hot pepper sauce

Serves 4

Place chicken in 8×8-in. dish. Add mushrooms. Cover with plastic wrap. Microwave at High 5 minutes.

In a small bowl, microwave butter at High 15 to 45 seconds. Blend in flour, salt and pepper. Stir in cream and sherry.

In small bowl, combine remaining ingredients. Add to cream mixture. Pour sauce over chicken breasts. Cover with plastic wrap. Reduce power to 50% (Medium). Microwave 5 to 9 minutes, or until meat is fork tender and no longer pink, rotating dish ½ turn after 3 minutes. Let stand 1 to 2 minutes.

Microwave	10¼-14¾
Standing	1-2 min.

Crab-Stuffed Chicken Breasts

- 1 can (5 oz.) crab meat, rinsed, drained and flaked
- ¼ cup chopped green onion
- 1 egg
- 1 tablespoon parsley flakes
- 2 teaspoons lemon juice
- ¼ teaspoon pepper
- 2 whole boneless chicken breasts, skinned and halved, lightly pounded
- 1 egg, beaten
- ⅓ cup seasoned bread crumbs

Serves 4

In small mixing bowl, combine all ingredients except chicken, egg and bread crumbs.

Place one-fourth of mixture on each half breast. Spread evenly. Roll breast up like a jelly roll. Dip each breast portion in egg and gently roll in bread crumbs to coat evenly.

Place rolls seam side down in 8×8-in. dish. Cover with wax paper. Microwave at High 6½ to 9½ minutes, or until chicken is fork tender, rotating dish after 4 minutes, and rearranging without turning over rolls.

Microwave 6½-9½ min.

◂ Crabmeat Canoes

- 2 medium zucchini, cut in half lengthwise
- ½ cup quick-cooking rice
- ¼ cup water
- 1 teaspoon instant chicken bouillon granules
- ½ teaspoon lemon juice
- 1 teaspoon parsley flakes
- ¼ teaspoon salt
- ⅛ teaspoon pepper
- 1 can (6½ oz.) crab meat, drained and rinsed
- ⅛ teaspoon paprika

Serves 4

Scoop out pulp from zucchini, leaving ¼ to ½-in. shell. Chop pulp coarsely. In 1-qt. casserole combine pulp and remaining ingredients except crab meat and paprika.

Microwave at High 4 to 6 minutes, or until rice is tender and moisture is absorbed. Stir in crab meat. Spoon filling into zucchini shells. Arrange in 8×8-in. baking dish. Sprinkle with paprika. Cover with wax paper.

Microwave at High 3 to 5 minutes, or until shells are tender, rotating dish ½ turn after half the cooking time.

Microwave	7-11 min.

Crab Newburg ▴

- 3 tablespoons butter or margarine
- 3 tablespoons flour
- 1¼ cups light cream
- 3 egg yolks, slightly beaten
- 1 can (5 oz.) crab meat, rinsed and drained
- 3 tablespoons white wine
- 2 teaspoons lemon juice
- ½ teaspoon salt
- 6 patty shells or toast points
- Paprika

Serves 4 to 6

In 1½-qt. casserole, microwave butter at High 30 to 60 seconds, or until melted. Stir in flour. Blend in cream with a wire whip. Microwave 2 minutes. Stir. Microwave 1 to 4 minutes, or until thickened, stirring after every minute.

Stir some of hot mixture into egg yolks. Blend egg yolks back into hot mixture. Microwave 1 to 1½ minutes, or until slightly thickened, stirring every 30 seconds.

Remove cartilage from crab. Stir crab meat into sauce. Microwave 1 to 1½ minutes, or until heated through.

Add wine, lemon juice and salt to crab mixture. Serve in patty shells or over toast points. Sprinkle with paprika.

Microwave	5½-10 min.

Shrimp Creole ▲

4 to 6 servings rice
½ cup chopped celery
½ cup chopped green pepper
½ cup chopped onion
1 clove garlic, minced
1 tablespoon olive oil
2 cans (16 oz. each) stewed tomatoes
¼ cup flour
1 teaspoon lemon juice
¼ teaspoon cayenne pepper
1 pkg. (12 oz.) frozen, quick-cooking shrimp, peeled and deveined

Serves 4 to 6

Cook rice conventionally while microwaving sauce.Combine celery, green pepper, onion, garlic and olive oil in 2-qt. casserole. Cover. Microwave at High 3 to 5 minutes, or until vegetables are tender.

Drain ⅓ cup liquid from tomatoes into 1-cup measure. Blend in flour until smooth. Add tomatoes with remaining juice, flour mixture, lemon juice and cayenne pepper to vegetables. Cover. Microwave 7 to 8 minutes, or until thickened.

Rinse shrimp in water to break apart. Stir into sauce. Cover. Reduce power to 50% (Medium). Microwave 10 to 15 minutes, or until shrimp are opaque, stirring three times. Serve over hot rice.

Microwave 20-28 min.

Shrimp in Buttery Sauce ▼

4 servings rice
¼ cup butter or margarine
¼ cup white wine
2 tablespoons lemon juice
1 tablespoon sugar
1 tablespoon cornstarch
1 teaspoon chopped chives
1 teaspoon parsley flakes
1 lb. fresh or defrosted shrimp

Serves 4

Cook rice conventionally while microwaving shrimp.

In 12x8-in. glass dish, melt butter at High 30 to 60 seconds. Blend in all ingredients except shrimp. Add shrimp and coat with sauce. Cover with wax paper. Microwave at High 4½ to 7½ minutes, or until shrimp are opaque, stirring after half the cooking time. Serve with rice.

Microwave 5-8½ min.

Stuffed Trout

2 whole trout (6 to 8 oz.), fresh or defrosted

Stuffing:

1/3 cup chopped celery
1/4 cup chopped onion
1/4 cup chopped green pepper
1/4 cup butter or margarine
1/2 cup seasoned bread crumbs
1/4 teaspoon lemon pepper

Sauce:

1 tablespoon butter or margarine
2 teaspoons lemon juice

Serves 2

In 1-qt. casserole combine celery, onion, green pepper and 1/4 cup butter. Cover; microwave at High 2 to 3 minutes, or until vegetables are tender.

Stir in bread crumbs and pepper. Stuff trout. If necessary, secure with wooden picks. Place in 8×8-in. baking dish.

In small dish melt 1 tablespoon butter at High 15 to 30 seconds. Mix in lemon juice.

Brush fish with lemon-butter. Cover dish with wax paper. Microwave at High 5 to 6 minutes, or until fish flakes easily, turning and brushing with lemon-butter after half the time.

Microwave	7 1/4-9 1/2 min.

Scallops & Green Beans

1 pkg. (9 oz.) frozen French style green beans
1/2 cup cornflake crumbs
1/4 cup grated Parmesan cheese
1 teaspoon parsley flakes
1/2 teaspoon salt
Dash pepper
Dash garlic powder
1 tablespoon butter or margarine
1 egg, slightly beaten
1 lb. scallops, fresh or defrosted
1 can (8 oz.) sliced water chestnuts, drained
1/8 teaspoon paprika

Serves 4

Microwave green beans in package at High 2 to 3 minutes, or until defrosted. Drain; set aside.

On wax paper combine crumbs, cheese, parsley and seasonings. Set aside, reserving 1 tablespoon for vegetables.

Melt butter in small dish at High 30 to 45 seconds. Blend with egg. Dip scallops in egg mixture. Coat well with crumbs. Arrange scallops around outside of roasting rack. Combine beans and water chestnuts. Mound in center of scallops. Sprinkle with reserved crumbs and paprika. Microwave 5 to 8 1/2 minutes, or until scallops are opaque, rotating dish after half the time.

Defrost	2-3 min.
Microwave	5 1/2-9 1/4 min.

Torsk Au Gratin

1 lb. torsk, fresh or defrosted, cut into 4-in. pieces

Sauce:

2 tablespoons butter or margarine
2 tablespoons flour
¼ teaspoon salt
⅛ teaspoon pepper
Dash nutmeg
1 cup milk or ½ cup milk and ½ cup light cream

Topping:

1 tablespoon butter or margarine
3 tablespoons dry bread crumbs
½ teaspoon parsley flakes

Serves 2

Microwave	10¼-13¼ min.

How to Microwave Torsk Au Gratin

Arrange torsk in 8×8-in. dish. Cover with plastic wrap. Microwave at High 5 to 6 minutes, or until fish flakes easily; rotate dish ½ turn after half the time. Set aside.

Melt butter at High 30 to 45 seconds in 1-qt. casserole. Stir in flour and seasonings. Blend in milk.

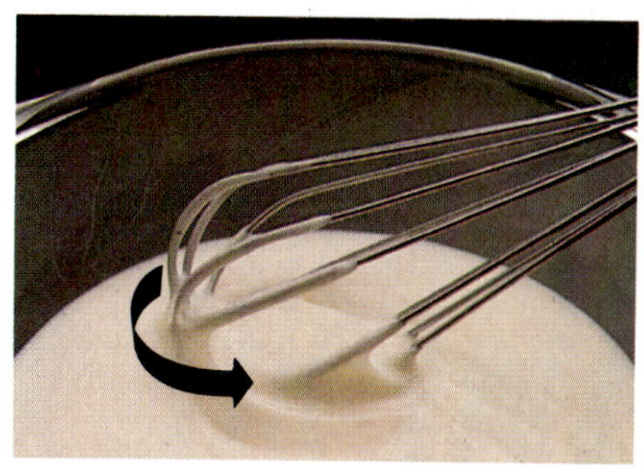

Microwave at High 3 to 4 minutes, or until thickened, stirring every minute. Set aside.

Melt butter for topping in small dish at High 15 to 30 seconds. Stir in bread crumbs and parsley flakes. Set aside.

Drain fish well. Break into bite size pieces. Add to sauce; mix gently until combined.

Sprinkle with topping. Microwave at High 1½ to 2 minutes, or until thoroughly heated.

◄Fish & Pepper Cups

- 2 small green peppers
- ⅔ cup diced zucchini
- ⅓ cup chopped tomato
- 2 tablespoons chopped onion
- ¼ teaspoon basil
- ¼ teaspoon salt
- Dash pepper
- ¾ cup crushed round buttery crackers
- ½ teaspoon dry mustard
- 1 teaspoon parsley flakes
- 1 lb. fish fillets, fresh or defrosted
- 1 tablespoon lemon juice

Serves 4

Cut peppers in half crosswise. Remove seeds. In small bowl, combine zucchini, tomato, onion, basil, salt and pepper. Spoon one-fourth of mixture into each pepper half. Set aside.

On wax paper, blend crackers, mustard and parsley flakes. Brush fillets with lemon juice. Coat with cracker mixture. Place fillets in center of roasting rack, with thickest portions to outside.

Place peppers around outer edge of rack. Microwave at High 6 to 9½ minutes, or until fish flakes easily, rotating dish and turning peppers around after 4 minutes. Top peppers with remaining crumbs before serving.

NOTE: Vegetables will be tender-crisp; for softer vegetables, microwave at High 1 minute after removing fish fillets.

Microwave 6-9½ min.

Sweet & Sour Fillets

- 1 lb. fish fillets, fresh or defrosted
- 3 tablespoons brown sugar
- 1 tablespoon cornstarch
- 1 teaspoon chives
- ¼ teaspoon dry mustard
- 1 can (8 oz.) pineapple chunks, drained and juice reserved
- 2 tablespoons vinegar
- 1 tablespoon soy sauce
- 1 pkg. (1¼ oz.) cashews

Serves 4

Arrange fillets in 12×8-in. baking dish. Cover with vented plastic wrap. Microwave at High 6 to 7 minutes, or until fish flakes easily, rotating dish ½ turn after half the cooking time. Set aside.

In 1-qt. casserole combine brown sugar, cornstarch, chives and dry mustard. Stir in pineapple juice, vinegar and soy sauce. Microwave at High 1½ to 2 minutes, or until thickened, stirring once or twice during cooking. Stir in pineapple chunks and cashews.

Drain fish well. Spoon sauce over. Microwave uncovered at High 1 to 2 minutes, or until thoroughly heated.

Microwave 8½-11 min.

Saucy Stuffed Fillets

¼ cup bread crumbs
¼ cup chopped green onion
1 can (5 oz.) drained, rinsed and flaked crab meat
1 egg, slightly beaten
1 teaspoon lemon juice
Dash cayenne
1 lb. fish fillets, fresh or defrosted*
2 tablespoons melted butter or margarine
Parsley flakes

Sauce:

1 cup sour cream
1 teaspoon dry mustard
1 teaspoon salt
½ teaspoon sugar
1 tablespoon pickle relish

Serves 4

Thoroughly combine crumbs, onion, crab meat, egg, lemon juice and cayenne. Spread on fillets; roll up and secure with picks. Arrange fillets in 8×8-in. dish. Brush with butter.

Microwave stuffed fillets at High 5 to 7 minutes, or until fish flakes easily, rotating once. Remove picks. Garnish with parsley.

Combine sauce ingredients in serving dish. Serve hot or cold.

*Long, thin fillets work most successfully.

Microwave	5-7 min.

Poached Fish & ► Mushrooms

2 tablespoons chopped onion
1 tablespoon butter or margarine
2 tablespoons white wine
½ teaspoon salt
¼ teaspoon sugar
¼ teaspoon tarragon
Dash pepper
1 lb. fish fillets, fresh or defrosted
8 oz. sliced fresh mushrooms

Serves 2 to 3

Place onion and butter in 12×8-in. baking dish. Microwave at High 1 to 1½ minutes, or until onion is translucent.

Stir in wine, salt, sugar, tarragon and pepper. Add fillets, turning to coat well with sauce. Top with mushrooms. Cover with plastic wrap.

Microwave at High 6 to 8 minutes, or until fish flakes easily. Rotate dish ½ turn and spoon sauce over mushrooms after half the cooking time.

Microwave	7-9½ min.

◄ Salmon Ring

- 2 tablespoons butter or margarine
- 3 tablespoons flour
- ½ cup milk
- 2 eggs
- 1 can (15 oz.) salmon, skin and bones removed, meat flaked
- 2 teaspoons lemon juice
- Mixed vegetables, optional

Sauce: optional

- 1 cup catsup
- 2 to 3 teaspoons horseradish sauce
- 1 teaspoon lemon juice

Serves 4

In medium bowl, melt butter at High 30 to 45 seconds. Stir in flour. Blend in milk, eggs, salmon and lemon juice. Pour into ring mold. Reduce power to 50% (Medium). Microwave 10 to 15 minutes, or until set, rotating dish twice. Cover tightly with foil. Let stand 7 to 10 minutes. Cook vegetables while ring stands.

Combine sauce ingredients in small bowl. Serve ring with sauce and mixed vegetables.

Microwave	10½-15¾ min.
Standing	7-10 min.

◄ Tuna & Shrimp Casserole

- 2 tablespoons butter or margarine
- 2 tablespoons flour
- ½ teaspoon salt
- ¼ teaspoon dry mustard
- ⅛ teaspoon pepper
- 1 cup milk
- ½ cup shredded Cheddar cheese
- 1 can (6½ oz.) chunk light tuna, drained
- 1 can (4½ oz.) tiny shrimp, drained
- 1 can (4 oz.) mushroom stems and pieces, drained
- 1 stalk celery, thinly sliced
- ¼ cup chopped onion
- ½ medium green pepper, cut into ¼ × 1-in. strips
- 2 cups chow mein noodles
- ¼ cup sliced almonds

Serves 4

In 1-qt. casserole melt butter at High 30 to 45 seconds. Blend in flour, salt, mustard and pepper. Stir in milk. Microwave 4½ to 7 minutes, or until thickened, stirring every minute. Stir in cheese until melted. Add tuna, shrimp and mushrooms.

Place celery, onion and green pepper in 2-qt. casserole. Cover. Microwave 2½ to 3½ minutes, or until tender-crisp. Stir in cheese sauce. Microwave uncovered 2½ to 3½ minutes, or until thoroughly heated. Stir in chow mein noodles. Sprinkle with almonds.

Microwave 10-14¾ min.

Tuna Medley ►

- 2 cups shredded carrots
- ½ cup thinly sliced celery
- ⅓ cup chopped onion
- 1 can (10¾ oz.) cream of mushroom soup
- 1 can (6½ oz.) chunk tuna, drained
- ½ pkg. (5 oz.) frozen green peas
- 1 teaspoon soy sauce
- 1 teaspoon parsley flakes
- ⅛ teaspoon garlic powder
- ⅛ teaspoon pepper
- 2 cans (1½ oz. each) shoestring potatoes, divided
- ½ cup cashews

Serves 4

Combine carrots, celery and onion in 2-qt. casserole. Cover. Microwave at High 3 to 4½ minutes, or until tender-crisp. Stir in soup, tuna, peas, soy sauce and seasonings. Cover. Microwave 4 to 6 minutes, or until thoroughly heated, stirring after half the cooking time.

Stir in two-thirds of the potatoes. Microwave 30 to 60 seconds. Sprinkle remaining potatoes and cashews over top.

Microwave 7½-11½ min.

Broccoli Quiche

1 pie shell (9-in.), baked, cooled
1 pkg. (10 oz.) broccoli cuts
3 eggs, slightly beaten
⅓ cup milk
1 can (3 oz.) French fried onion rings, divided
1 cup shredded Cheddar cheese, divided
½ teaspoon salt
⅛ teaspoon pepper

Serves 4 to 6

Defrost broccoli in package at High 3½ to 4 minutes. Drain.

In medium mixing bowl beat egg and milk; stir in broccoli, ½ can onion rings, ½ cup cheese, salt and pepper. Pour into pie shell. Microwave at 50% (Medium) 8 to 15 minutes, or until almost set, rotating ¼ turn every 4 minutes.

Sprinkle remaining onion rings and cheese over top. Microwave at 50% (Medium) 1½ to 2½ minutes, or until cheese melts. Let stand 5 minutes.

Defrost	3½-4 min.
Microwave	9½-17½ min.
Standing	5 min.

Sweet Potato Puff

¼ cup butter or margarine
¼ cup flour
½ teaspoon salt
⅛ teaspoon cinnamon
Dash nutmeg
1 cup milk
¼ cup brown sugar
1 cup mashed, cooked sweet potatoes or yams (can be canned or precooked)
4 eggs, separated
1 teaspoon cream of tartar
2 tablespoons chopped pecans, optional

Serves 2 to 4

In 2-qt. casserole microwave butter at High 30 to 45 seconds, or until melted. Blend in flour and seasonings. Slowly stir in milk.

Microwave at High 3 to 3½ minutes, or until thickened, stirring every minute. Add brown sugar, sweet potatoes or yams and slightly beaten egg yolks.

In large mixing bowl beat egg whites with cream of tartar until stiff peaks form. Gently fold egg whites into thickened sauce.

Microwave at 50% (Medium) 15 to 19 minutes, or until top edges appear dry and center seems set, rotatinig ¼ turn about every 3 minutes. Sprinkle with pecans, if desired.

Microwave	18½-23¼ min.

Spanish Scrambled Eggs

- ½ cup chopped green pepper
- 1 tablespoon butter or margarine
- 6 beaten eggs
- 2 tablespoons milk
- ½ teaspoon salt
- ¼ teaspoon pepper
- ¼ teaspoon oregano leaves
- ½ cup finely chopped, peeled, seeded tomato
- ½ cup shredded mozzarella or ¼ cup grated Parmesan

Serves 2 to 3

In 1-qt. casserole, combine green pepper and butter. Microwave covered at High 1½ to 2½ minutes, or until butter is melted and green pepper is hot.

In small bowl, blend eggs, milk, salt, pepper and oregano. Mix into green pepper. Microwave 3½ to 5 minutes, or until eggs are soft and moist, stirring and pushing cooked portions to center after 2 minutes, 1 minute, then every 30 seconds.

Stir in tomatoes. Cover. Let stand covered 1 minute. If desired, sprinkle on, or stir in cheese and allow to stand covered 1 to 2 more minutes.

Microwave	5-7½ min.
Standing	2-3 min.

Denver Sandwiches

- 3 tablespoons chopped green pepper
- 2 tablespoons chopped onion
- 2 teaspoons butter or margarine
- 3 eggs
- ½ cup fully cooked chopped ham
- 1 tablespoon milk
- ⅛ teaspoon dry mustard
- ⅛ teaspoon salt
- ⅛ teaspoon pepper
- Bread or toast

Serves 4

Combine green pepper, onion and butter in small mixing bowl. Microwave at High 1 to 2½ minutes, or until vegetables are tender.

Stir in eggs, chopped ham, milk and seasonings. Pour into two small saucers. Microwave at High 2 to 5 minutes, or until eggs are almost set, pushing cooked portions toward center of dish and rotating saucers once or twice during cooking.

Serve open face or as sandwiches with bread or toast.

Microwave	3-7½ min.

Spaghetti Carbonara

1 pkg. (7 oz.) spaghetti
10 slices bacon
3 tablespoons butter or margarine
¾ cup grated Parmesan cheese
3 eggs

Serves 4

Cook spaghetti conventionally while microwaving bacon.

Arrange bacon on paper towels or on a rack in baking dish. Cover with paper towels. Microwave at High 8 to 10 minutes, or until bacon is almost crisp. Let stand 3 to 5 minutes. Crumble.

In 2-qt. casserole, microwave butter at High 45 to 60 seconds, or until melted. Mix in cheese, eggs and bacon.

Drain spaghetti; add to casserole. Toss with cheese mixture.

Microwave at High 2 to 4 minutes, or until eggs are set, tossing every minute.

Microwave	10¾-15 min.
Standing	3-5 min.

Macaroni & Cheese

1 pkg. (5 oz.) spiral macaroni
3 tablespoons butter or margarine
3 tablespoons flour
1 teaspoon chives
½ teaspoon salt
⅛ teaspoon white pepper
⅛ teaspoon cayenne
1½ cups milk
1 cup shredded Cheddar cheese
1 cup shredded white cheese, such as Monterey Jack
1½ tablespoons seasoned bread crumbs

Serves 6

Cook macaroni conventionally while microwaving sauce. In 2-qt. casserole melt butter at High 45 to 60 seconds. Stir in flour and seasonings until smooth. Microwave at High 30 to 45 seconds, or until bubbly. Blend in milk. Microwave at High 4 to 7 minutes, or until thickened, stirring every minute.

Mix in cheeses until melted; if needed, microwave at High 30 seconds. Stir in macaroni. Microwave at High 3 minutes. Stir; sprinkle with bread crumbs. Microwave at High 2 minutes, or until thoroughly heated.

Variation:
Add ½ to 1 cup cooked cubed meat (such as ham, pork or chicken) with macaroni.

Microwave	10¾-14¼ min.

Mexican Lasagna

1½ tablespoons minced onion
1 tablespoon dehydrated green pepper
3 tablespoons water
2 tablespoons butter or margarine
1 can (4 oz.) diced green chilies, drained
3 eggs
1 cup small-curd creamed cottage cheese
½ teaspoon salt
½ teaspoon oregano
¼ teaspoon ground cumin
⅛ teaspoon pepper
4 cups broken tortilla chips, divided
2 cups shredded Monterey Jack cheese, divided
1½ cups shredded Cheddar cheese, divided
1 cup sour cream

Serves 4 to 6

NOTE: For a "hotter" casserole Jalapeno peppers can be added as a garnish with the tortilla chips.

Microwave	19-27 min.
Standing	3 min.

How to Microwave Mexican Lasagna

Combine onion, green pepper, water and butter in 2-qt. casserole or medium bowl. Microwave at High 2 to 3 minutes, or until vegetables are rehydrated. Stir in green chilies. Set aside.

Mix together eggs, cottage cheese and seasonings. Sprinkle 1½ cups chips over bottom of 12×8-in. dish. Spoon half of cottage cheese mixture over chips.

Spread half of onion mixture over cottage cheese. Sprinkle with 1½ cups Monterey Jack and 1 cup Cheddar cheese. Repeat chips, cottage cheese and onion layers.

Swiss Eggs

8 slices bacon
1/3 cup chopped green pepper
1/4 cup chopped onion
1 tablespoon butter or margarine
8 eggs
3 tablespoons milk
1/2 teaspoon salt
Dash pepper
1 cup shredded Swiss cheese

Serves 4 to 6

Microwave bacon on roasting rack or paper towels at High 6 to 8 minutes, or until crisp, rotating once after 3 minutes. Crumble and set aside.

In glass cake dish, combine vegetables and butter. Microwave at High 45 seconds to 1¼ minutes, or until butter melts.

In medium mixing bowl, blend eggs, milk, salt and pepper. Add to vegetables in cake dish. Stir in bacon. Microwave 3 to 6 minutes, stirring after 2 minutes and then after every minute to break up cooked portions, until eggs are almost set, but still coated with moisture. Stir; sprinkle with cheese. Reduce power to 50% (Medium). Microwave 30 to 45 seconds to soften cheese. Cover with dinner plate. Let stand 3 to 5 minutes to set eggs and melt cheese.

Microwave	10¼-16 min.
Standing	3-5 min.

Microwave at High 5 minutes. Reduce power to 50% (Medium). Microwave 9 to 14 minutes, or until center is almost set, rotating dish after half the cooking time.

Combine remaining cheeses and sour cream. Spread over casserole. Sprinkle with remaining chips.

Microwave at High 3 to 5 minutes, or until sour cream is heated, rotating dish after half the cooking time. Let stand 3 minutes before serving.

Hearty "Meal" Soups & Sandwiches

A substantial soup or sandwich can make a satisfying meal. Each of these recipes contains sufficient protein to qualify as a main dish. For a balanced meal, add a salad of crisp greens or fresh fruit.

New England Clam Chowder

4 slices bacon, cut into eighths
3 cups potatoes peeled and cut into ¼-in. cubes
1 medium onion, chopped
2 cans (6½ oz.) minced clams, drained and liquid reserved
¼ cup flour
2 cups milk, divided
1½ teaspoons salt
⅛ teaspoon pepper
⅔ cup light cream

Serves 4

Microwave 20-26 min.

How to Microwave New England Clam Chowder

Place bacon in 3-qt. casserole. Cover; microwave at High 3 minutes. Drain all but 2 tablespoons fat.

Add potatoes and onion. Pour reserved clam liquid into casserole. Cover.

Microwave at High 7 to 9 minutes, or until potatoes are fork tender, stirring once.

Easy Split Pea Soup

- 2 medium carrots, thinly sliced
- 1 small onion, chopped
- 1 medium potato, peeled and cut into ½-in. cubes
- ¾ cup hot water
- 1 can (11½ oz.) split pea soup
- ¾ cup milk
- 1 to 1½ cups cooked, cubed ham
- ¼ teaspoon marjoram
- ⅛ teaspoon pepper

Serves 4

In 2-qt. casserole combine carrots, onion, potato and water. Cover. Microwave at High 5 minutes, or until vegetables are tender-crisp. Add soup, milk, ham and seasonings to vegetables. Microwave at High 5 to 10 minutes, or until soup is thoroughly heated.

Microwave 10-15 min.

Combine flour and ¼ cup milk. Add flour mixture, remaining milk, salt and pepper to casserole. Do not cover.

Microwave at High 8 to 10 minutes, or until thickened, stirring several times.

Stir in clams and light cream. Microwave at High 2 to 4 minutes, or until heated through.

Creamy Beef & Sausage Soup

½ lb. ground beef, crumbled
½ lb. ground sausage*, crumbled
1 medium onion, thinly sliced and separated into rings
1 stalk celery, sliced
1 cup thinly sliced carrots
2½ cups hot water, divided
1 can (15 oz.) great northern beans
1 can (10¾ oz.) cream of celery soup
1 pkg. (9 oz.) frozen cut green beans
1 teaspoon salt
1 teaspoon parsley flakes
½ teaspoon basil
1 bay leaf

Serves 4

*Mild flavored ground sausage works best.

Microwave 22-30 min.

How to Microwave Creamy Beef & Sausage Soup

Combine ground beef and sausage in 3-qt. casserole. Microwave at High 4 to 6 minutes, or until meat is no longer pink. Drain meat on paper towels. Discard fat.

Combine onion, celery, carrots and 1 cup water in casserole. Cover. Microwave at High 8 to 11 minutes, or until vegetables are tender.

Add meat, 1½ cups water and remaining ingredients to vegetables. Cover tightly. Microwave at High 10 to 13 minutes, or until thoroughly heated, stirring after half the cooking time.

Stuffed Tomatoes

4 medium, ripe tomatoes
2 cups coarsely chopped fresh mushrooms
⅓ cup chopped celery
¼ cup chopped onion
3 tablespoons butter or margarine
⅓ cup fine dry bread crumbs
¼ teaspoon salt
¼ teaspoon dried thyme
1 egg, slightly beaten
1 cup shredded Cheddar cheese, divided

Serves 2

Microwave	8-9 min.
Standing	1-2 min.

How to Microwave Stuffed Tomatoes

Remove stem ends of tomatoes; scoop out pulp and seeds. Place tomatoes in 8×8-in. baking dish. Set aside.

Combine mushrooms, celery, onion and butter in 1-qt. casserole. Microwave at High 4 to 4½ minutes, or until celery is tender-crisp. Stir in bread crumbs, seasonings, egg and ¾ cup cheese.

Spoon stuffing into tomatoes. Cover dish with plastic wrap. Microwave at High 4 to 4½ minutes, or until tomatoes are tender, rotating dish ½ turn after half the cooking time.

Sprinkle remaining cheese over stuffed tomatoes, re-cover and let stand 1 to 2 minutes, or until cheese melts.

Hamburger-Vegetable Soup

1 lb. lean ground beef
1 medium potato, peeled and cut into ¼-in. cubes
1½ cups shredded cabbage
3 cups hot water
1 can (16 oz.) whole tomatoes
1 pkg. (10 oz.) frozen mixed vegetables
1 tablespoon instant beef bouillon granules
2 tablespoons minced onion
1 tablespoon parsley flakes
1 teaspoon Worcestershire sauce
½ teaspoon salt

Serves 4

Crumble ground beef into 3-qt. casserole. Mix in potato and cabbage. Cover. Microwave at High 5 to 7 minutes, or until meat is no longer pink, stirring once.

Add remaining ingredients. Cover. Microwave 17 to 22 minutes, or until potatoes are tender, stirring once.

Microwave	22-29 min.

Leftover Chicken & Noodle Soup

2 cups cooked, cubed chicken
2½ cups hot water
1½ cups fine egg noodles
1 cup frozen mixed vegetables
2 teaspoons chives
⅛ teaspoon marjoram
Dash pepper
1 tablespoon instant chicken bouillon granules

Serves 4

Combine all ingredients in 3-qt. casserole. Cover. Microwave at High 12 to 15 minutes, or until noodles are tender, stirring frequently during cooking.

Microwave	12-15 min.

Tomato, Hamburger and Rice Soup

½ lb. ground beef
3 tablespoons flour
2 cups tomato juice
½ cup quick-cooking rice
2 tablespoons sugar
1¼ teaspoons salt
¼ teaspoon onion powder
⅛ teaspoon pepper
1 bay leaf
1½ cups milk

Serves 4

Crumble ground beef into 2-qt. casserole. Microwave at High 1½ to 2 minutes, or until meat is no longer pink, stirring after half the cooking time. Drain.

Stir in flour. Mix in tomato juice, rice, sugar, seasonings and bay leaf. Cover. Microwave at High 5 to 6 minutes, or until rice is tender, stirring twice during cooking.

Slowly blend in milk. Microwave uncovered at High 3 to 5 minutes, or until hot, stirring once during cooking.

Microwave 9½-13 min.

◂Beefy Spaghetti Soup

- ½ lb. ground beef, crumbled
- 1 medium onion, chopped
- ⅛ teaspoon garlic powder
- ¾ cup chopped celery
- 1 teaspoon olive oil
- 2 cups hot water
- 1 can (10½ oz.) beef consomme
- 2 cups sliced fresh mushrooms
- 1 cup frozen cut green beans
- 1½ cups broken spaghetti (uncooked)
- 1 teaspoon instant beef bouillon granules
- 1 teaspoon parsley flakes
- ¾ teaspoon salt
- ⅛ teaspoon pepper
- 1 bay leaf
- 1 can (8 oz.) tomato sauce
- ½ teaspoon oregano

Serves 4

In 3-qt. casserole combine ground beef, onion, garlic, celery and oil. Microwave at High 2½ to 3½ minutes, or until meat is no longer pink, stirring once during cooking. Drain.

Add remaining ingredients. Cover. Microwave at High 17 to 20 minutes, or until spaghetti is tender, stirring occasionally.

Microwave 19½-23½ min.

Beef & Vegetable Soup

- 2 medium carrots, thinly sliced
- 1 large potato, peeled and cut into ½-in. cubes
- 1 medium onion, sliced
- 1 cup sliced celery
- 1½ cups hot water
- 1½ cups cooked cubed beef
- 2 tablespoons flour
- 1 can (8 oz.) tomato sauce
- 2 teaspoons instant beef bouillon granules
- ½ teaspoon salt
- ¼ teaspoon basil
- ⅛ teaspoon pepper
- 1 cup frozen peas

Serves 6

In 3-qt. casserole combine carrots, potato, onion, celery and water. Cover. Microwave at High 8 to 10 minutes, or until vegetables are tender, stirring after half the cooking time.

In a small bowl toss beef cubes with flour to coat. Combine with tomato sauce, bouillon granules, seasonings, peas and vegetables. Cover. Microwave at High 7 to 9 minutes, or until thoroughly heated.

Microwave 15-19 min.

Chili Burgers

1 lb. ground beef
1 cup chopped celery
½ cup chopped onion
½ cup chopped green pepper
1 can (10¾ oz.) tomato soup
¼ cup catsup
1 tablespoon brown sugar
1 teaspoon chili powder
½ teaspoon dry mustard
1 teaspoon salt
⅛ teaspoon cayenne
⅛ teaspoon pepper
⅛ teaspoon garlic powder
1 tablespoon cornstarch
1 can (15 oz.) kidney beans, drained

Serves 4

In 2-qt. casserole combine ground beef, celery, onion and green pepper. Cover. Microwave at High 5 to 6 minutes, or until meat is no longer pink, stirring after half the cooking time to break up meat. Drain.

Stir in remaining ingredients. Cover. Microwave at High 5 minutes. Stir. Reduce power to 50% (Medium). Microwave 7 to 10 minutes to blend flavors.

Serve in hamburger buns.

Microwave 17-21 min.

Ham or Beef Open-Face Barbecue Sandwiches

4 slices bread
8 to 10 oz. thinly sliced, cooked ham or beef

Sauce:
½ cup catsup
1 can (4 oz.) mushroom stems and pieces, drained
2 tablespoons brown sugar
1 teaspoon vinegar
½ teaspoon prepared mustard
Dash chili powder
Dash ground cloves

Serves 2

Toast bread conventionally. Halve each slice and arrange on roasting rack. Layer ham or beef evenly on toast. Let stand while preparing sauce.

In 2-cup measure, combine sauce ingredients. Microwave at High 2 to 3½ minutes, or until hot and bubbly, stirring once or twice during cooking.

Pour sauce evenly over meat. Microwave at 50% (Medium) 2½ to 4 minutes, or until thoroughly heated, rotating dish after half the cooking time.

Microwave 4½-7½ min.

Tuna-Cheese Open-Face Sandwich

1 can (6½ oz.) tuna, drained
2 hard cooked eggs, peeled and chopped
¼ cup salad dressing or mayonnaise
¼ cup finely chopped onion
2 tablespoons sweet relish
2 tablespoons chopped stuffed olives or celery
½ teaspoon prepared mustard
½ teaspoon salt
⅛ teaspoon pepper
4 English muffins or hamburger buns, split and toasted
8 slices tomato
½ cup shredded American or Cheddar cheese

Serves 4

In medium bowl combine tuna, eggs, salad dressing, onion, relish, olives, mustard, salt and pepper. Spoon about ¼ cup mixture onto each muffin half. Top with 1 slice tomato and 1 tablespoon cheese.

Place 4 open-face sandwiches on plate lined with two layers of paper towels. Microwave at High 2 to 3 minutes, or until cheese melts, rotating dish once or twice during cooking. Repeat with remaining sandwiches.

Microwave 2-3 min.

30 Minute Meals
With Make-Ahead Mixes

30 Minute Meals From Make-Ahead Mixes

These easy to fix beef, pork, and chicken mixtures get you started on a variety of 30 minute meals. Prepare one on a weekend or free evening. Divide the basic mixture into packages as directed, then freeze for future quick meals. A package of mix takes about 10 minutes to defrost; you can use that time to assemble the remaining ingredients for the recipe you've selected, prepare a mixed green salad to complement the meal and set the table. Of course, you can use one package the day you make the mix, or refrigerate it for use the next day. That way, you'll save even more time.

Basic Beef Mix

4 medium onions, sliced
3 cloves of garlic, minced
3 tablespoons olive oil
5 lbs. lean* ground beef
1 bottle (12 oz.) chili sauce
1 envelope (.75 oz.) onion soup mix
1 envelope (.75 oz.) brown gravy mix
2 teaspoons salt

Makes 5 packages

*If using less lean beef, skim fat after cooking.

Defrost	8-11 min.
Microwave	22½-29½ min.

How to Microwave Basic Beef Mix

Combine onions, garlic, and oil in 5-qt. casserole. Cover. Microwave at High 3½ to 5½ minutes, or until onions are tender-crisp, stirring once or twice.

Crumble ground beef into onion mixture. Cover. Microwave 14 to 16 minutes, or until meat loses its pink color, stirring 2 or 3 times.

Stir in remaining ingredients. Cover. Microwave at High 5 to 8 minutes.

Spaghetti Beef Mix

6 servings spaghetti
1 pkg. basic beef mix, defrosted
1 can (15 oz.) tomato puree
1 can (6 oz.) tomato paste
½ cup water
2 teaspoons Italian seasoning
½ teaspoon basil
½ teaspoon salt
¼ teaspoon sugar
⅛ teaspoon pepper
1 small bay leaf

Serves 4 to 6

Cook spaghetti conventionally while microwaving sauce. Combine all ingredients in 2-qt. casserole. Microwave at High 5 minutes. Stir. Reduce power to 50% (Medium). Microwave 20 minutes to allow flavors to blend. Serve over hot spaghetti.

Microwave	25 min.

How to Freeze & Defrost Basic Beef Mix

To freeze: divide cooked mixture into 5 containers (approx. 2⅓ cups each). Cover. Label and freeze.

To defrost: place 1 package beef mix in container called for in recipe you plan to use.

Microwave at 50% (Medium) 8 to 11 minutes, or until defrosted, breaking apart with a fork once or twice.

Chili

- 1 pkg. basic beef mix, defrosted
- 1 can (16 oz.) tomato sauce
- 1 can (16 oz.) kidney beans, drained
- 1½ to 2 teaspoons chili powder
- ½ teaspoon crushed red pepper, optional

Serves 4 to 6

In 2-qt. casserole, combine all ingredients. Cover. Microwave at High 6 to 10 minutes, or until hot and bubbly, stirring once. Serve with crackers or topped with cheese.

Defrost	8-11 min.
Microwave	6-10 min.

Stroganoff

- 4 to 6 servings rice or noodles
- 1 pkg. basic beef mix, defrosted
- 1 can (4 oz.) button mushrooms, drained
- ½ cup cool water
- 3 tablespoons flour
- 2 teaspoons instant beef bouillon granules
- 1 teaspoon Worcestershire sauce
- 6 oz. cream cheese

Serves 4 to 6

Cook rice or noodles conventionally while microwaving sauce.

In 1½-qt. casserole, combine beef mix and mushrooms. Stir flour into water until smooth. Blend flour mixture, bouillon and Worcestershire sauce into meat mixture.

Microwave at High 3 to 6 minutes, or until hot and thickened. Stir in cream cheese until melted. If necessary, microwave at High ½ to 1½ minutes, or until heated. Serve over rice or noodles.

Defrost	8-11 min.
Microwave	3½-7½ min.

Lasagna

4 lasagna noodles, divided
1 pkg. basic beef mix, defrosted
½ cup chopped green pepper
1 can (8 oz.) tomato sauce
1 can (6 oz.) tomato paste
½ teaspoon oregano
1 bay leaf
1 pkg. (15 oz.) ricotta cheese, divided
4 tablespoons Parmesan cheese, divided
1 cup (4 oz.) shredded mozzarella cheese

Serves 4

Cook noodles conventionally while microwaving sauce.

In medium mixing bowl or 1½-qt. casserole, combine beef mix, green pepper, tomato sauce, tomato paste, oregano and bay leaf. Cover loosely. Microwave at High 10 minutes, or until hot and bubbly. Remove bay leaf.

See photo directions below to assemble and microwave Lasagna.

Defrost	8-11 min.
Microwave	21-24 min.

How to Microwave Lasagna

Place half of the noodles on the bottom of an 8×8-in. dish. Top with half of beef mixture.

Spread two-thirds of ricotta over meat and top with half the Parmesan cheese. Repeat with remaining noodles, beef mixture and ricotta. Sprinkle with mozzarella. Top with remaining Parmesan cheese.

Microwave at High 5 minutes, rotating ½ turn after 3 minutes. Reduce power to 50% (Medium). Microwave 6 to 9 minutes, or until hot and bubbly.

Layered Casserole

2 to 2½ cups mashed potatoes, warm, as directed on page 132
1 pkg. basic beef mix, defrosted
1 can (10½ oz.) vegetable or vegetable beef soup, divided
3 tablespoons flour
1 teaspoon instant beef bouillon, optional
1 pkg. (10 oz.) frozen peas
½ cup shredded Cheddar cheese
1 egg
1 teaspoon parsley flakes
⅛ teaspoon paprika

Serves 4

Defrost	8-11 min.
Microwave	21½-27½ min.

How to Microwave Layered Casserole

Place beef mix in 8×8-in. dish. Defrost if needed as directed on page 87. Pour one-fourth of soup into beef mix.

Stir flour and bouillon into remaining soup. Blend soup mixture into meat. Microwave at High 3 minutes.

Microwave peas in package at High 3½ to 4½ minutes, or until package is warm. Drain well.

Spread peas over beef mixture. Blend cheese, egg, parsley and paprika into potatoes.

Pipe or spread potatoes evenly over peas. Microwave at High 5 minutes, rotating once.

Reduce power to 50% (Medium). Microwave 10 to 15 minutes, or until heated through, rotating once or twice.

Stuffed Green Peppers

1 pkg. basic beef mix, defrosted
1¼ cups quick-cooking rice
1 can (8 oz.) tomato sauce
½ teaspoon basil leaves
½ teaspoon salt
⅛ teaspoon pepper
4 large green peppers
⅓ cup grated Cheddar cheese, optional

Serves 4

In medium mixing bowl combine beef mix, rice, tomato sauce, basil, salt and pepper. Remove tops, pulp and seeds from peppers. Fill each with one-fourth of beef mixture. Place in 8×8-in. baking dish. Cover with plastic wrap. Microwave at High 10 to 15 minutes, or until peppers are tender and rice is rehydrated. If desired, top with cheese during last minute of cooking. Let stand covered 3 minutes.

Defrost	8-11 min.
Microwave	10-15 min.
Standing	3 min.

Make-Ahead Pork Mix

Basic Pork Mix

3 lbs. boneless pork, cut into ½-in. cubes
2 medium onions, chopped
1 cup thinly sliced celery
1 pkg. (¾ oz.) pork gravy mix
2 tablespoons flour
¼ cup water
1 tablespoon instant chicken bouillon granules
1 teaspoon salt
1 teaspoon bouquet sauce
¼ teaspoon pepper
1 bay leaf

Makes 3 packages

Defrost	9-12 min.
Microwave	25-35 min.
Standing	5 min.

How to Microwave Basic Pork Mix

Toss meat and vegetables with gravy mix and flour in 3 to 5-qt. casserole.

Add remaining ingredients. Cover. Microwave at High 10 minutes. Stir; re-cover. Reduce power to 50% (Medium).

Microwave 15 to 25 minutes, or until pork is fork tender, stirring twice during cooking. Let stand 5 minutes.

How to Freeze & Defrost Basic Pork Mix

To freeze: divide mix into thirds, package in shallow freezer boxes or heat-sealable bags and freeze.

To defrost: place 1 package pork mix in 1-qt. casserole.

Microwave at 50% (Medium) 9 to 12 minutes, or until defrosted, breaking apart with fork after first 5 minutes, then after 3 minutes.

Pork Chop Suey ▲

- ¼ cup water or dry white sherry
- 3 tablespoons soy sauce
- 1 tablespoon cornstarch
- 1 cup sliced celery
- 1 tablespoon butter or margarine
- 1 pkg. basic pork mix, defrosted
- 1 can (16 oz.) chop suey (or mixed chinese) vegetables, drained
- 1 can (8½ oz.) bamboo shoots, drained
- ½ cup chopped green onions
- 4 servings chow mein noodles

Serves 4

In 1-cup measure combine water, soy sauce and cornstarch. Microwave at High 1 to 2 minutes or until thick, stirring once during cooking. Set aside.

In 2-qt. casserole microwave celery and butter at High 2 to 2½ minutes or until tender-crisp. Stir in thickened sauce and remaining ingredients except chow mein noodles.

Microwave at High 6 to 9 minutes or until thoroughly heated, stirring after half the cooking time. Serve over chow mein noodles.

Defrost	9-12 min.
Microwave	9-13½ min.

Pork & Sauerkraut ►

- 2 medium apples, chopped (about 2½ cups)
- 1 tablespoon butter or margarine
- 1 tablespoon flour
- 1 pkg. basic pork mix, defrosted
- 1 can (16 oz.) sauerkraut, rinsed and well drained
- 4 tablespoons brown sugar, divided
- ½ teaspoon caraway seed
- ⅓ cup chopped pecans

Serves 4

In 2-qt. casserole combine apples and butter. Cover; microwave at High 2 to 3 minutes or until tender. Remove half the mixture to a small bowl; set aside.

Stir flour into remaining mixture, then add pork mix, sauerkraut, 2 tablespoons brown sugar and caraway seed. Cover; microwave at High 5 to 6 minutes or until heated through, stirring after half the cooking time.

Combine reserved apple-butter mixture with 2 tablespoons brown sugar and pecans. Sprinkle over pork and sauerkraut. Microwave uncovered at High 1 to 3 minutes, or until topping melts.

Defrost	9-12 min.
Microwave	8-12 min.

Pork & Refried Bean Enchiladas

8 corn tortillas*

Filling:
- 1 pkg. (1 lb.) basic pork mix, defrosted
- 1 can (16 oz.) refried beans
- 1 teaspoon chili powder
- ¼ teaspoon tabasco sauce
- ⅛ teaspoon garlic powder

Sauce:
- 3 tablespoons butter or margarine
- 3 tablespoons flour
- ½ teaspoon salt
- ½ teaspoon dry mustard
- Dash cayenne pepper
- 1½ cups milk

Topping:
- ½ cup shredded Monterey Jack cheese
- ½ cup shredded Cheddar cheese
- ⅛ teaspoon paprika

Serves 4 to 8

*To make rolling easier, soften by dipping in a little water or oil, then blot dry with paper towels.

Defrost	9-12 min.
Microwave	15½-24 min.

How to Microwave Pork & Refried Bean Enchiladas

Combine filling ingredients in 2-qt. casserole. Cover; microwave at High 5 to 8 minutes, or until thoroughly heated, stirring after half the time. Set aside.

Microwave butter at High 60 seconds in 1½-qt. casserole until melted. Stir in flour and seasonings. Blend in milk.

Microwave at High 4½ to 6 minutes, or until thickened, stirring after 2 minutes, and then every minute.

Spread ⅓ cup filling down center of each tortilla while sauce is cooking. Roll up; arrange seam side down in 12×8-in. dish.

Pour thickened sauce evenly over enchiladas. Microwave at High 2 to 5 minutes, or until heated through.

Sprinkle with cheeses and paprika. Reduce power to 50% (Medium). Microwave 3 to 4 minutes or until cheese melts.

Make-Ahead Chicken Mix

Basic Chicken Mix

8½ to 9 lbs. chicken pieces, such as drumsticks, thighs and split breasts
¼ cup flour
1 large onion, chopped
1 small carrot, finely chopped
2 tablespoons instant chicken bouillon granules
1 tablespoon parsley flakes
1 teaspoon salt
½ teaspoon basil
½ teaspoon marjoram
¼ teaspoon pepper

Makes 4 packages

Microwave	35-50 min.
Defrost	6-12 min.

How to Microwave Basic Chicken Mix

Combine chicken pieces and flour in 4 to 5-qt. casserole , adding chicken in layers and sprinkling each layer with some of the flour. Add remaining ingredients. Cover.

Microwave at High 35 to 50 minutes, or until meat is no longer pink, stirring pieces frequently during cooking.

Quick Chicken Pilaf

½ cup chopped celery
½ cup chopped green pepper
2 teaspoons olive oil
1 pkg. basic chicken mix, defrosted
2 cups instant or quick-cooking rice
1 cup hot water
1 teaspoon instant chicken bouillon granules
1 teaspoon chives
¼ teaspoon salt
1 bay leaf
⅓ cup seedless raisins, optional
½ cup cashews

Serves 4

In 2-qt. casserole combine celery, green pepper and olive oil. Cover. Microwave at High 1½ to 2½ minutes or until tender.

Stir in remaining ingredients except raisins and nuts. Cover. Microwave at High 7 to 10 minutes or until rice is tender and liquid is absorbed. Stir in raisins, if desired. Sprinkle with cashews. Let stand covered 2 to 3 minutes.

Defrost	6-12 min.
Microwave	8½-12½ min.
Standing	2-3 min.

How to Freeze & Defrost Basic Chicken Mix

Cool slightly to make handling easier. Remove meat from bones. Cut into bite size pieces; return to sauce in casserole.

To freeze: divide evenly into 4 portions (about 2 cups each). Package in shallow freezer boxes or heat-sealable bags.

To defrost: place mixture in small bowl. Microwave at 50% (Medium) 6 to12 minutes, stirring occasionally to break up.

Chicken Stew With Dumplings

- 1 pkg. basic chicken mix, defrosted
- 3 tablespoons flour
- 3 medium carrots, thinly sliced (about 1½ cups)
- 2 large potatoes, peeled and cut into ½-in. cubes (about 3½ cups)
- 1 can (10¾ oz.) chicken broth
- ¼ cup water
- ½ teaspoon salt
- ⅛ teaspoon rosemary
- ⅛ teaspoon pepper
- 1 cup frozen peas

Dumplings:

- 1½ cups buttermilk baking mix
- 2 teaspoons poppy seeds
- 1 teaspoon parsley flakes
- ½ cup milk
- 1 teaspoon wheat germ

Serves 4

Defrost	6-12 min.
Microwave	26-35 min.

How to Microwave Chicken Stew With Dumplings

Toss chicken mix with flour in 3-qt. casserole. Add remaining stew ingredients except peas. Cover. Microwave at High 20 to 25 minutes, or until vegetables are tender, stirring once.

Stir in frozen peas. Re-cover. Microwave at High 2 to 4 minutes, or until peas are tender. Prepare dumplings while stew is cooking.

Combine buttermilk baking mix, poppy seeds, parsley flakes and milk. Drop 8 tablespoonfuls in a ring on top of stew. Sprinkle dumplings with wheat germ if desired.

Microwave at High 4 to 6 minutes, or until dumplings are set, rotating dish ½ turn after half the cooking time.

Chicken Casserole

1½ cups frozen cut green beans
1½ cups frozen cauliflowerets
2 tablespoons water
1 pkg. basic chicken mix, defrosted
1½ cups cooked macaroni
1 cup shredded Cheddar cheese, divided
1 can (10¾ oz.) cream of mushroom soup
1 teaspoon parsley flakes
1 teaspoon lemon juice
½ teaspoon poultry seasoning
½ teaspoon dry mustard
½ teaspoon salt
⅛ teaspoon pepper
1 tablespoon dry bread crumbs

Serves 4

In 2-qt. casserole combine green beans, cauliflowerets and water. Microwave uncovered at High 6 to 9 minutes or until tender. Drain. Cut large cauliflowerets into smaller pieces.

Stir in chicken, macaroni, ¾ cup cheese, soup, parsley, lemon juice and seasonings. Microwave uncovered at High 7 minutes. Stir.

Sprinkle bread crumbs and remaining cheese over top. Microwave at High 2 to 3½ minutes, or until heated through and cheese is melted.

Defrost	6-12 min.
Microwave	15-19½ min.

Chicken & Broccoli Over Spaghetti ►

1 pkg. (6 to 7 oz.) spaghetti, cooked & drained
1 pkg. (10 oz.) frozen chopped broccoli
¼ cup butter or margarine
¼ cup flour
¾ teaspoon salt
½ teaspoon onion powder
⅛ teaspoon pepper
Dash garlic powder
2½ cups milk
1 pkg. basic chicken mix, defrosted
¼ cup grated Parmesan cheese

Serves 4 to 6

Defrost	6-12 min.
Microwave	16-23 min.

How to Microwave Chicken & Broccoli Over Spaghetti

Cook spaghetti conventionally while microwaving sauce. Microwave broccoli in package at High 4 to 6 minutes or until tender. Drain and set aside. Place butter in 2-qt. casserole.

Melt butter at High 60 seconds. Stir in flour, seasonings, then milk. Microwave at High 6 to 11 minutes, or until thickened, stirring several times. Add broccoli and chicken.

Place spaghetti in 12×8-in. dish. Pour on sauce evenly. Sprinkle with Parmesan cheese. Microwave at High 5 minutes, or until heated through, rotating dish ½ turn after half the time.

◄ Chicken Paprikash

- 1 clove garlic, pressed or minced
- 2 cups sliced fresh mushrooms
- 1 cup sliced celery
- 1 medium onion, sliced
- 1 tablespoon butter or margarine
- 1 pkg. basic chicken mix, defrosted
- 1½ teaspoons paprika
- ½ teaspoon sugar
- ½ cup sour cream

Serves 4

In 1½ to 2-qt. casserole combine garlic, mushrooms, celery, onion and butter. Cover; microwave at High 3 to 5 minutes or until tender. Drain.

Mix in remaining ingredients except sour cream. Cover; microwave at High 2 to 5 minutes, or until thoroughly heated, stirring once during cooking.

Blend in sour cream. Reduce power to 50% (Medium). Microwave 30 seconds to 1½ minutes to heat through, if needed.

Defrost	6-12 min.
Microwave	5½-11½ min.

30 Minutes Plus

30 Minutes Plus

The main dishes in this section take about 30 minutes to microwave. The "plus" is the time needed to prepare ingredients. This takes additional time, but there are several things you can do to speed preparation.

If you have a food processor, chopping and slicing take only seconds. If you prepare ingredients by hand, do it in the morning or the night before, or ask someone else in the household to help.

These recipes include a starch or a vegetable, so once the main dish is in the oven, you'll have time to make a salad and prepare a dessert to microwave while the family is at the table.

Overnight Marinated West Coast Round Steak

- 1½ to 2 lbs. boneless round steak, ¼ to ½-in. thick
- 1 cup teriyaki sauce
- 1 cup water
- ⅓ cup barbecue sauce
- Butter or margarine
- 1 medium onion, sliced & separated into rings

Serves 4

Cut steak into serving size pieces, removing excess fat. Pound both sides with meat mallet or edge of saucer.

Place meat in baking dish. Combine teriyaki sauce, water and barbecue sauce. Pour over meat. Let stand covered in refrigerator overnight, turning meat once or twice.

Preheat browning dish at High 5 minutes. Add butter and steak. Microwave at High 15 seconds; turn steak pieces over. Add onions. Cover. Reduce power to 50% (Medium). Microwave 12 to 18 minutes, or until meat is fork tender, turning meat once. Let stand 5 to 10 minutes.

Microwave	17¼-23¼ min.
Standing	5-10 min.

Overnight Marinated Stuffed Flank Steak

1 to 1½ lb. flank steak
1 can (8 oz.) tomato sauce
1 envelope onion soup mix
1 teaspoon Worcestershire sauce
1 cup shredded potato
½ cup chopped green onion
1 can (8 oz.) cut green beans, drained

Serves 4

Microwave	27-33½ min.
Standing	5-10 min.

How to Microwave Overnight Marinated Stuffed Flank Steak

Pound flank steak well with mallet or saucer edge to flatten and tenderize. Combine tomato sauce, soup mix and Worcestershire sauce in 2-cup measure.

Spread half of tomato mixture in 8×8-in. dish. Place meat over mixture. Top with remaining tomato mixture. Cover. Marinate in refrigerator overnight.

Scrape marinade from both sides of meat and dish into 2-cup measure. Microwave at High 1 to 1½ minutes, or until hot.

Combine potatoes and green onions in small bowl. Microwave at High 1 to 2 minutes, or until hot. Stir in beans. Spread vegetable mixture on flank steak.

Roll meat up like jelly roll, securing with wooden picks. Place seam side up in 8×8-in. dish. Top with marinade. Cover with plastic wrap. Microwave at High 5 minutes.

Reduce power to 50% (Medium). Microwave 20 to 25 minutes, or until meat is fork tender, turning seam side down and basting with marinade after 10 minutes. Let stand 5 to 10 minutes.

◄ Beef Strips in Tomato Sauce

4 to 6 servings noodles, rice or toast points
1 to 1¼ lb. boneless beef top round steak, ½-in. thick, pounded and cut into very thin strips
¼ cup flour
1 envelope onion soup mix
1 can (16 oz.) stewed tomatoes
1 can (8 oz.) tomato sauce
1 tablespoon parsley flakes

Serves 4 to 6

Prepare noodles, rice or toast points conventionally while microwaving beef.

In 2-qt. casserole, toss together meat, flour and soup mix. Stir in remaining ingredients. Microwave at High 5 minutes. Stir.

Reduce power to 50% (Medium). Microwave 15 to 20 minutes, or until meat is tender, stirring after half the cooking time.

Stir and let stand 5 minutes. Serve over toast points, noodles or rice.

Microwave	20-25 min.
Standing	5 min.

Overnight Marinated ▲ Teriyaki Strips

1½ to 2 lbs. top round steak, cut in thin strips
1 cup teriyaki marinade
4 to 6 servings rice or chow mein noodles
1 tablespoon cooking oil
8 oz. fresh mushrooms, sliced
1 medium onion, sliced and separated into rings
2 tablespoons cornstarch dissolved in 2 tablespoons cold water

Serves 4 to 6

Combine meat and marinade in deep bowl or plastic bag. Marinate overnight in refrigerator.

Cook rice, if desired, using your favorite method.

Drain meat. Preheat 10-in. browning dish at High 6 minutes. Add oil and meat. Stir once or twice until sizzling stops. Stir in remaining ingredients. Cover. Microwave at High 7 to 11 minutes, or until meat is cooked and sauce is glossy, stirring 2 or 3 times. Serve over rice or chow mein noodles.

Microwave	13-17 min.

Pepper Steak Strips

- 4 servings rice
- 1½ lbs. boneless beef round steak, ½-in. thick
- ¼ cup soy sauce
- 1 tablespoon paprika
- 2 tablespoons butter or margarine
- 1 medium green pepper, cut into thin strips
- 1 stalk celery, thinly sliced
- 1 clove garlic, minced or pressed
- ½ cup water, divided
- 1½ tablespoons cornstarch
- 1 cup green onion cut into ½-in. pieces
- 1 medium tomato, peeled and cut into chunks

Serves 4

Microwave	21-26½ min.

How to Microwave Pepper Steak Strips

Cook rice conventionally. Trim fat from steak; pound to ¼-in. thickness with meat mallet. Cut into ¼-in. wide strips. Combine strips, soy sauce and paprika.

Set aside while preparing other ingredients. Preheat browning dish at High 5 minutes. Add butter and drained beef strips.

Microwave at High 2½ to 3½ minutes, or until meat is browned, stirring once. Add green pepper, celery, garlic and ¼ cup water. Cover.

Reduce power to 50% (Medium). Microwave 11 to 14 minutes, or until meat is tender and vegetables are tender-crisp, stirring once during cooking.

Combine cornstarch and remaining water. Add to meat mixture with onions and tomato. Increase power to High.

Microwave uncovered 2½ to 4 minutes, or until sauce is thickened, stirring once during cooking. Serve over rice.

Italian Meatloaf

1½ lbs. lean ground beef
½ cup dry bread crumbs
1 can (8 oz.) tomato sauce, divided
1 egg
1 teaspoon oregano, divided
1 teaspoon salt
⅛ teaspoon pepper
1½ cups shredded mozzarella cheese
2 tablespoons grated Parmesan cheese

Serves 4 to 6

Mix together ground beef, bread crumbs, half the tomato sauce, egg, ½ teaspoon oregano, salt and pepper. On wax paper, pat into a rectangle ½-in. thick. Sprinkle with mozzarella.

Roll up by starting on short side. Lift paper until meat begins to roll tightly. Peel back paper to keep it free. Continue lifting and peeling to complete roll. Seal edges and place in loaf dish.

Microwave at High 9 minutes, rotating dish after half the cooking time.

Reduce power to 50% (Medium). Microwave 11 to 14 minutes, or until meat loses most of its pink color, rotating dish after half the cooking time. Drain.

Combine remaining tomato sauce and oregano. Pour over meatloaf. Sprinkle with Parmesan. Microwave 2 minutes to heat sauce.

Tent with foil and let stand 5 minutes before serving.

Microwave	22-25 min.
Standing	5 min.

Four-Layer Dinner

- 1 pkg. (10 oz.) frozen chopped spinach
- 2 cups cooked rice
- 1 cup shredded Swiss cheese, divided
- 1 egg, beaten
- 1 lb. ground beef
- 1 can (6 oz.) tomato paste
- 1 envelope (¾ oz.) mushroom gravy mix
- ⅔ cups water
- ¼ teaspoon basil

Serves 4 to 6

Variation:

Layered Broccoli Bake: Substitute 1 pkg. (10 oz.) frozen chopped broccoli for frozen spinach.

Microwave	20½-27½ min.

How to Microwave Four-Layer Dinner

Microwave spinach in package at High 3 to 4 minutes, or until defrosted. Drain. Set aside. Place rice in 12×8-in. dish. Microwave at High 1½ to 2 minutes, or until heated. Stir in ½ cup cheese and egg. Press mixture evenly into bottom of dish.

Microwave 3 to 4 minutes, or until set; rotate dish after 2 minutes. Crumble ground beef into 2-qt. casserole. Microwave 3½ to 5 minutes, or until meat loses its pink color, stirring once. Drain fat. Blend in remaining ingredients except spinach.

Spoon meat over rice. Spread spinach evenly over meat. Top with remaining cheese. Microwave 5 minutes. Rotate dish ½ turn. Reduce power to 50% (Medium). Microwave 4½ to 7½ minutes, or until heated.

◂ Meatballs with Potatoes & Carrots

- 4 medium carrots, thinly sliced
- 1 large potato, peeled and cut into ½-in. cubes
- 1 medium onion, thinly sliced
- 2 tablespoons water
- 1 tablespoon instant beef bouillon granules
- 2 teaspoons parsley flakes
- 1 bay leaf
- 1 lb. lean ground beef
- ¼ cup dry bread crumbs
- 1 egg
- 1 teaspoon bouquet sauce
- 1 teaspoon salt
- ¼ teaspoon dry mustard
- ⅛ teaspoon garlic powder
- ⅛ teaspoon pepper

Serves 4

In 12×8-in. baking dish combine vegetables, water, bouillon granules, parsley flakes, and bay leaf. Cover with plastic wrap. Microwave at High 3 minutes.

While microwaving vegetables, mix remaining ingredients. Shape into 14 to 16 meatballs.

Arrange meatballs on top of vegetables. Re-cover. Microwave 11 to 15 minutes, or until vegetables are tender, stirring after half the cooking time.

Microwave 14-18 min.

Meatballs on Rice ▴

- 1 lb. ground beef
- ¾ cup chopped onion, divided
- ¼ cup dry bread crumbs
- 1 egg
- 3 tablespoons soy sauce, divided
- 1 teaspoon seasoned salt
- 2 cups sliced fresh mushrooms
- ½ cup chopped celery
- 2 cups quick-cooking rice
- 1 can (10½ oz.) cream of mushroom soup
- 1 cup water

Serves 4

Combine ground beef, ¼ cup onion, bread crumbs, egg, 1 tablespoon soy sauce and seasoned salt. Shape into 20 to 25 meatballs.

Place in 12×8-in. baking dish. Microwave at High 5 to 6 minutes, or until set, but meat is still pink, rearranging after half the time.

Drain meatballs on paper towels. Add remaining onion, mushrooms and celery to dish. Cover with plastic wrap. Microwave at High 4 to 7 minutes, or until tender. Drain all but 2 tablespoons fat from dish.

Mix in remaining soy sauce, rice, soup and water. Arrange meatballs on top. Re-cover. Microwave at High 5 to 7 minutes, or until rice is tender and liquid is absorbed, pushing rice at edge of dish toward center after half the cooking time.

Microwave 14-20 min.

Sweet & Sour Meatballs

4 to 5 servings rice or chow mein noodles
Water
2 cans (8¼ oz. each) chunk pineapple, reserve juice
¾ cup brown sugar
¼ cup cornstarch
¾ cup cider vinegar
⅓ cup soy sauce
½ lb. ground beef
½ lb. lean ground pork
1 egg, beaten
3 tablespoons soy sauce
¼ cup dry bread crumbs
1 green pepper, thinly sliced

Serves 4 to 5

Microwave	17½-25 min.

How to Microwave Sweet & Sour Meatballs

Cook rice conventionally. Add enough water to pineapple juice to equal 1⅓ cups. In 2-qt. casserole, combine with brown sugar, cornstarch, vinegar, and soy sauce.

Microwave at High 7½ to 11 minutes, or until mixture is thick and glossy, stirring twice with wire whip. Set aside.

Combine beef, pork, egg, soy sauce and bread crumbs in medium mixing bowl. Form into 20 meatballs. Place meatballs and green pepper in 12×8-in. dish.

Place meatballs in oven. Microwave at High 6 to 8 minutes, or until meat loses pink color, stirring once to rearrange.

Drain fat from meatballs. Add meatballs, green pepper and pineapple to sauce.

Microwave 4 to 6 minutes, or until hot, stirring once. Serve over rice or chow mein noodles.

◄ Pork Chops & Saucy Vegetables

1 pkg. (9 oz.) frozen cut green beans
1 can (16 oz.) bean sprouts, drained
1 can (10¾ oz.) cream of chicken soup
1 can (8 oz.) sliced water chestnuts, drained
1 can (3 oz.) French fried onion rings, divided
¾ teaspoon salt
¼ teaspoon ginger
⅛ teaspoon pepper
4 pork chops, ½ to ¾-in. thick, trim excess fat if desired

Serves 4

Microwave green beans in package at High 3 to 4 minutes or until defrosted.

In 12×8-in. dish, combine bean sprouts, soup, green beans, water chestnuts, half the onion rings and seasonings. Top with pork chops, placing meatiest portions to outer edge of dish. Cover with plastic wrap.

Microwave at High 7 minutes. Rearrange and turn chops over; stir vegetables. Re-cover. Reduce power to 50% (Medium). Microwave 10 to 20 minutes or until meat is no longer pink, rotating dish ½ turn after half the cooking time. Uncover.

Sprinkle chops with remaining onion rings. Microwave at High 1 to 2 minutes to heat through.

Microwave	21-33 min.

Pork Chops With Creamy Rice & Peas ▲

1 can (10¾ oz.) cream of mushroom soup
½ cup sour cream
½ teaspoon salt
¼ teaspoon ginger
¼ teaspoon rosemary leaves, crushed
1 pkg. (10 oz.) frozen peas
1 can (4 oz.) mushroom stems and pieces, drained
1 can (3 oz.) French fried onion rings, divided
½ cup instant or quick-cooking rice
4 pork chops, ½-in. thick

Serves 4

In medium bowl blend soup, sour cream and seasonings. In 12×8-in. dish combine three-fourths of soup mixture with peas, mushrooms, half the onion rings and rice.

Arrange pork chops on top with meatiest portions to outside of dish. Spoon remaining sauce over chops. Cover with wax paper. Microwave at High 10 minutes. Rotate dish. Reduce power to 50% (Medium). Microwave 12 to 17 minutes, or until meat loses almost all its pink color, turning chops over and stirring vegetable mixture after half the cooking time.

Sprinkle onion rings over chops. Increase power to High. Microwave 3 minutes to finish cooking.

Microwave	25-30 min.

Pork Chops, Sauerkraut & Potatoes

2 cups shredded potatoes
1 small onion, chopped
1 can (1 lb.) sauerkraut, drained
1 can (10¾ oz.) cream of chicken soup, divided
2 tablespoons brown sugar
½ teaspoon caraway seed
½ teaspoon salt
⅛ teaspoon pepper
4 pork chops, ½-in. thick
1 teaspoon bouquet sauce
1 teaspoon water
3 tablespoons milk

Serves 4

Combine potatoes and onion in 12×8-in. dish. Cover with plastic wrap. Microwave at High 4 to 6 minutes, or until potatoes are tender. Stir in sauerkraut, two-thirds of soup, sugar, caraway seed, salt and pepper. Spread evenly in dish. Arrange chops on top with meatiest portions to outside of dish. Combine bouquet sauce and water. Brush chops with half of mixture.

Microwave at High uncovered 17 to 21 minutes, or until chops lose their pink color, turning over and brushing chops with bouquet mixture after half the cooking time. Let stand covered while preparing sauce.

Combine remaining soup and milk in 1-cup measure. Microwave at High 1½ to 3 minutes to heat. Serve with chops.

Microwave	22½-30 min.

Stuffed Pork Chops & Brussels Sprout Dinner

1 cup chopped, unpeeled, apple (1 medium apple)
¼ cup raisins
2 teaspoons grated orange peel
⅛ teaspoon ground cinnamon
1 tablespoon butter or margarine
½ cup dry bread crumbs (seasoned preferred, not necessary), divided
2 teaspoons packed brown sugar
8 pork chops, ¼-in. thick
1 pkg. (10 oz.) frozen Brussels sprouts (or cooking bag Brussels sprouts)

Serves 4

Microwave 18-27 min.

How to Microwave Stuffed Pork Chops & Brussels Sprout Dinner

Combine apple, raisins, orange peel, cinnamon and butter in 2-cup measure. Microwave at High 2 to 4 minutes, or until apples are tender. Stir in ¼ cup bread crumbs and brown sugar. Place one-fourth of stuffing mixture (approx. ¼ cup) on each pork chop.

Top each pork chop with another chop. Secure with wooden picks. Coat chops with ¼ cup bread crumbs. Arrange chops on outer edges of roasting rack in baking dish. Microwave Brussels sprouts in package at High 3 to 4 minutes, or until slightly warm. Remove from package; wrap in plastic wrap, leaving thickness of no more than 2 sprouts.

Microwave chops 5 minutes. Place wrapped sprouts in center of roasting rack. Reduce power to 50% (Medium). Microwave 10 to 16 minutes, or until meat is no longer pink and sprouts are tender, rearranging after 8 minutes.

Pork Chops & ▲ Stuffed Tomatoes

- 1/3 cup seasoned dry bread crumbs
- 1/2 teaspoon ground thyme
- 4 pork chops, 1/2-in. thick
- 1 egg, lightly beaten
- 4 medium tomatoes
- 1 cup frozen peas
- 1 teaspoon butter or margarine
- 1/2 teaspoon basil leaves, optional
- 2 teaspoons Parmesan cheese

Serves 4

Combine bread crumbs and thyme. Dip pork chops in egg. Dredge in bread crumbs. Place chops on roasting rack with meatiest portions to outside. Microwave at High 5 minutes.

Remove stem ends from tomatoes; scoop out pulp and seeds. To stuff each tomato: fill with 1/4 cup frozen peas. Dot with 1/4 teaspoon butter. Sprinkle with one-fourth of basil, and top each with one-fourth of cheese.

Place tomatoes on rack. Reduce power to 50% (Medium). Microwave 10 minutes.

Rearrange but don't turn over chops and tomatoes. Microwave at 50% (Medium) 8 to 11 minutes, or until chops are no longer pink and vegetables are tender.

Microwave	23-26 min.

Pork Chops on Fruit & ► Vegetable Stuffing

- 1 1/2 cups thinly sliced celery
- 3 cups chopped apples
- 1 medium onion, thinly sliced
- 1 cup herb-seasoned stuffing mix
- 1/4 cup raisins
- 1/4 teaspoon nutmeg
- 4 pork chops, 1/2-in. thick
- 1 tablespoon butter or margarine
- 1 tablespoon bouquet sauce

Serves 4

In 12×8-in. dish, microwave celery at High 1 1/2 to 3 1/2 minutes, or until tender-crisp. Add apples, onion, stuffing mix, raisins and nutmeg, tossing well to combine. Arrange pork chops on top of stuffing, with meatiest portions to outside of dish.

In 1-cup measure, microwave butter at High 30 to 45 seconds, or until melted. Stir in bouquet sauce. Brush chops with half the mixture. Cover with wax paper. Microwave 3 minutes.

Reduce power to 50% (Medium). Microwave 8 minutes. Turn over and rearrange chops. Stir stuffing to redistribute. Brush chops with remaining bouquet sauce mixture. Cover with wax paper. Microwave at 50%(Medium) 7 to 11 minutes, or until meat is no longer pink.

Microwave	20-26 1/4 min.

◂Barbecued Lamb Chops

1 small onion, chopped
1 tablespoon butter or margarine
¼ cup chili sauce
¼ cup catsup
3 tablespoons brown sugar
1 teaspoon vinegar
⅛ teaspoon garlic powder
4 lamb chops, 1½-in. thick

Serves 4

In 1-qt. casserole combine onion and butter. Microwave at High 1½ to 2 minutes, or until tender. Stir in remaining ingredients except chops.

Arrange chops on roasting rack with meatiest portions to outside. Spoon half of sauce over chops. Cover with wax paper. Microwave at High 3 minutes. Reduce power to 50% (Medium). Microwave 5 minutes.

Turn over and rearrange chops. Spoon on remaining sauce; re-cover. Microwave 10 to 20 minutes, or until chops are desired doneness.

Microwave 19½-30 min.

Orange Glazed Lamb Chops

⅓ cup orange marmalade
2 tablespoons honey
1 tablespoon prepared mustard
2 teaspoons lemon juice
1 teaspoon Worcestershire sauce
4 lamb chops, 1½-in. thick

Serves 2 to 4

Combine all ingredients except chops in 2-cup measure. Microwave at High 30 to 45 seconds, or until marmalade melts. Stir.

Arrange chops on roasting rack with meatiest portions to outside. Spoon half of glaze over chops. Cover with wax paper. Microwave at High 3 minutes. Reduce power to 50% (Medium). Microwave 5 minutes.

Turn over and rearrange chops. Spoon on remaining glaze. Re-cover. Microwave 10 to 20 minutes, or until chops are desired doneness.

Microwave 18½-28¾ min.

Overnight Marinated Lamb Kabobs

- 1 lb. lamb, cut into 20 cubes (1-in.)
- ¾ to 1 cup Italian salad dressing
- ½ medium green pepper, cut into 16 cubes (¾-in.)
- 8 medium fresh mushrooms
- 8 cherry tomatoes

Serves 4

Combine lamb and salad dressing. Cover. Refrigerate overnight.

On each of 4 skewers arrange kabobs as shown at right, reversing order for other half of skewer. Place kabobs on roasting rack. Cover with wax paper. Microwave at 50% (Medium) 5 minutes.

Turn over and rearrange. Microwave 4 to 8 minutes, or until lamb is tender. Green pepper will remain tender-crisp.

Microwave	9-13 min.

Lamb Stew

- 1 lb. lamb, cut into ½-in. cubes
- 2 tablespoons flour
- 1½ teaspoons salt
- 1 teaspoon parsley flakes
- ½ teaspoon marjoram
- ¼ teaspoon pepper
- ⅛ teaspoon garlic powder
- ¼ teaspoon thyme
- ¾ cup water
- ⅓ cup white wine
- ¼ teaspoon bouquet sauce
- 1 large potato, peeled and cut into ½-in. cubes
- 1 medium onion, thinly sliced
- 1 bay leaf
- 1 pkg. (10 oz.) frozen peas and carrots

Serves 4

In 3-qt. casserole toss lamb with flour and seasonings. Stir in water, wine and bouquet sauce. Add potato, onion and bay leaf. Cover. Microwave at High 10 minutes, stirring after half the cooking time.

Reduce power to 50% (Medium). Microwave covered 10 to 15 minutes, or until meat and potatoes are fork tender. Stir in peas and carrots. Cover. Microwave at 50% (Medium) 5 minutes, or until vegetables are heated. Let stand covered 5 minutes.

Microwave	25-30 min.
Standing	5 min.

Cabbage Rolls

8 cabbage leaves

Filling:

½ lb. ground sausage*, crumbled
1 medium onion, chopped
¼ teaspoon garlic powder
1 can (16 oz.) kidney beans, drained
1 carton (8 oz.) ricotta cheese
½ teaspoon salt

Sauce:

1 can (8 oz.) tomato sauce
1 teaspoon chili powder

*"Hot" sausage gives the rolls a spicy flavor; mild is also suitable.

Serves 4

Microwave whole cabbage at High 2 minutes, or until 8 outer leaves can be separated easily. Refrigerate remaining cabbage for future use.

See photo directions on page 39 for filling and rolling cabbage leaves.

Cut out hard center rib from each cabbage leaf. Place leaves in 12×8-in. baking dish. Cover with plastic wrap. Microwave at High 2 to 2½ minutes, or until leaves are pliable. Set aside.

In 1½ to 2-qt. casserole, combine sausage, onion and garlic. Microwave at High 2½ to 3 minutes, or until meat is no longer pink. Drain. Add remaining filling ingredients.

Spoon one-eighth filling mixture (about ⅓ cup) on base of each cabbage leaf. Fold in sides of leaf; roll up. Place seam side down, around edges of 12×8-in. dish.

Combine sauce ingredients; pour over rolls. Cover with wax paper. Microwave at High 6 to 10 minutes, or until filling is hot and cabbage is tender, rotating dish ½ turn two or three times during cooking.

Microwave	12½-17½ min.

Sausage & Spinach Noodle Casserole

2 cups spinach noodles
1 lb. ground pork sausage, crumbled
½ cup chopped onion
½ cup chopped celery
1 can (4 oz.) mushroom stems and pieces, drained
1 teaspoon salt
⅛ teaspoon pepper
1 cup shredded Muenster, Monterey Jack or other mild white cheese
¼ cup grated Parmesan cheese, divided
2 tablespoons milk

Serves 4

Cook spinach noodles conventionally while microwaving sausage.

Combine sausage, onion and celery in 2-qt. casserole. Microwave at High 7 to 9 minutes, or until sausage loses its pink color and vegetables are tender, stirring to break up meat after half the cooking time. Drain and break up meat.

Stir in spinach noodles, mushrooms, salt and pepper. Add shredded cheese, 2 tablespoons Parmesan cheese and milk. Cover. Microwave at High 5 to 7 minutes, or until cheese melts, stirring after half the time.

Sprinkle with remaining Parmesan cheese before serving.

Microwave	12-16 min.

Wurst & German Potato Salad

1 cup water, divided
1½ teaspoons salt, divided
4 medium potatoes, peeled and cooked
4 slices bacon
½ cup chopped onion
¼ cup sugar
2 tablespoons flour
½ teaspoon celery seed
Dash pepper
½ cup cider vinegar
4 smoked bratwurst or knockwurst

Serves 4

Microwave 24½-32½ min.

How to Microwave Wurst & German Potato Salad

Combine ¼ cup water, ½ teaspoon salt and peeled, quartered potatoes. Cover. Microwave at High 9 to 12 minutes, or until fork tender, rearranging after half the cooking time. Drain and cut into chunks. Can be done the night before.

Place bacon on rack in 12×8-in. dish. Cover with paper towel. Microwave at High 3 to 4 minutes, or until crisp. Drain bacon on paper towels, reserving fat in dish.

Remove rack from dish. Add onion to bacon fat. Microwave 1½ to 2½ minutes, or until tender. Stir in sugar, flour, 1 teaspoon salt, celery seed and pepper.

Mix in ¾ cup water and vinegar. Microwave 5½ to 7 minutes, or until mixture thickens, stirring twice during cooking time. Crumble bacon into hot mixture.

Stir in potato chunks gently. Arrange wurst on top. Microwave 5½ to 7 minutes, or until wurst are hot, rearranging after half the cooking time.

Chicken Sauced With Peas & Carrots ▲

- 1 pkg. (10 oz.) frozen peas and carrots
- 1 can (10¾ oz.) cream of chicken soup
- ⅓ cup finely chopped onion
- 1 teaspoon poultry seasoning
- ½ teaspoon salt
- ⅛ teaspoon dry mustard
- 3 to 3½ lbs. broiler-fryer chicken pieces, skin removed if desired
- ½ cup dry white wine or chicken broth

Serves 4

Microwave peas and carrots in package at High 4 to 5 minutes, or until defrosted. Set aside.

In a 1-qt. measure combine soup, onion and seasonings. Arrange chicken pieces in 12×8-in. baking dish with meatiest portions to outside. Stir in wine. Pour soup mixture evenly over chicken. Cover dish with wax paper. Microwave at High 17 to 20 minutes, or until meat near bone is no longer pink, rotating dish ½ turn and stirring sauce gently after half the cooking time.

Remove chicken to serving plate; skim fat if needed. Cover. Stir peas and carrots into sauce. Microwave uncovered at High 2 to 5 minutes, or until vegetables are tender. Serve vegetable sauce with chicken.

Microwave	23-30 min.

Chicken & Broccoli Plate ►

- 6 chicken thighs
- 1 envelope onion soup mix
- 1 small head broccoli
- ¼ cup water

Serves 4 to 6

Skin chicken, if desired. Coat with onion soup mix. Arrange chicken along outer edges of microwave baking sheet.

Cut 2 to 3 inches from tough end of broccoli. Cut tender ends into spears. Place broccoli in center of baking sheet with tops toward center of sheet. Sprinkle with water. Cover broccoli only with plastic wrap. Microwave at High 18 to 27 minutes, or until broccoli is tender and chicken near bone is no longer pink, rotating dish ½ turn after 10 minutes. Let stand 1 to 2 minutes.

Microwave	18-27 min.
Standing	1-2 min.

Chicken With Sour Cream & Chive Potatoes ►

- 1 pkg. (4¾ oz.) sour cream and chive potatoes
- 2 cups hot water
- 2 tablespoons butter or margarine
- ⅔ cup milk
- 2 to 3 lbs. broiler-fryer chicken pieces, skin removed if desired
- 2 teaspoons butter, melted
- 1 teaspoon bouquet sauce
- 1 teaspoon chives

Serves 4

In 12×8-in. dish combine potatoes and seasonings from mix, water and butter. Cover with vented plastic wrap. Microwave at High 10 minutes. Stir in milk.

Place chicken pieces on top of potatoes, bony side up and meatiest portions to outer edges of dish. Combine melted butter and bouquet sauce. Brush chicken with mixture. Re-cover. Microwave at High 10 minutes.

Turn over and rearrange chicken pieces. Brush chicken with bouquet sauce mixture; sprinkle with chives. Re-cover. Microwave at High 6 to 10 minutes, or until meat is no longer pink and potatoes are tender.

Microwave	26-30 min.

Chicken & Mushroom Stuffing

2 cups fresh sliced mushrooms
½ cup chopped onion
½ cup chopped celery
¼ cup butter or margarine
⅓ cup hot water
3 cups cubed herb-seasoned stuffing
1 egg
½ teaspoon instant chicken bouillon granules
½ teaspoon salt, divided
⅓ cup seasoned dry bread crumbs
1 teaspoon parsley flakes
2½ to 3 lbs. broiler-fryer chicken pieces, skin removed if desired

Serves 4

Microwave	18½-25 min.

How to Microwave Chicken & Mushroom Stuffing

Combine mushrooms, onion, celery and butter in 12×8-in. dish. Cover with wax paper. Microwave at High 2 to 4 minutes or until tender.

Measure water into 1-cup measure. Microwave at High 30 to 60 seconds, or until boiling. Add stuffing, water, egg, bouillon and ¼ teaspoon salt to mushroom mixture. Stir.

Combine bread crumbs, parsley and ¼ teaspoon salt on wax paper. Coat chicken with crumbs. Place on stuffing with meatiest portions to outside of dish. Cover with wax paper.

Microwave at High 10 minutes. Rearrange pieces but do not turn over. Re-cover. Microwave at High 6 to 10 minutes, or until meat is no longer pink. Remove to platter. Serve with stuffing.

Apricot Glazed Turkey Legs

½ cup apricot preserves
2 tablespoons brown sugar
1 tablespoon prepared mustard
½ teaspoon Worcestershire sauce
2 turkey legs (1¾ to 2 lbs.)

Serves 2 to 4

In 1-cup measure combine all ingredients except turkey legs. Microwave at High 1 minute, or until thoroughly heated.

Place turkey legs on roasting rack, with meatiest portions to outer edges. Spoon on one-third of the glaze. Cover with wax paper. Microwave at High 3 minutes.

Reduce power to 50% (Medium). Microwave 12 minutes. Turn legs over and spoon on another one-third of the glaze. Re-cover. Microwave at 50% (Medium) 6 to 16 minutes, or until juices run clear and meat is no longer pink.

Spoon on remaining glaze. Microwave at 50% (Medium) 1 to 3 minutes to heat glaze.

Microwave 23-35 min.

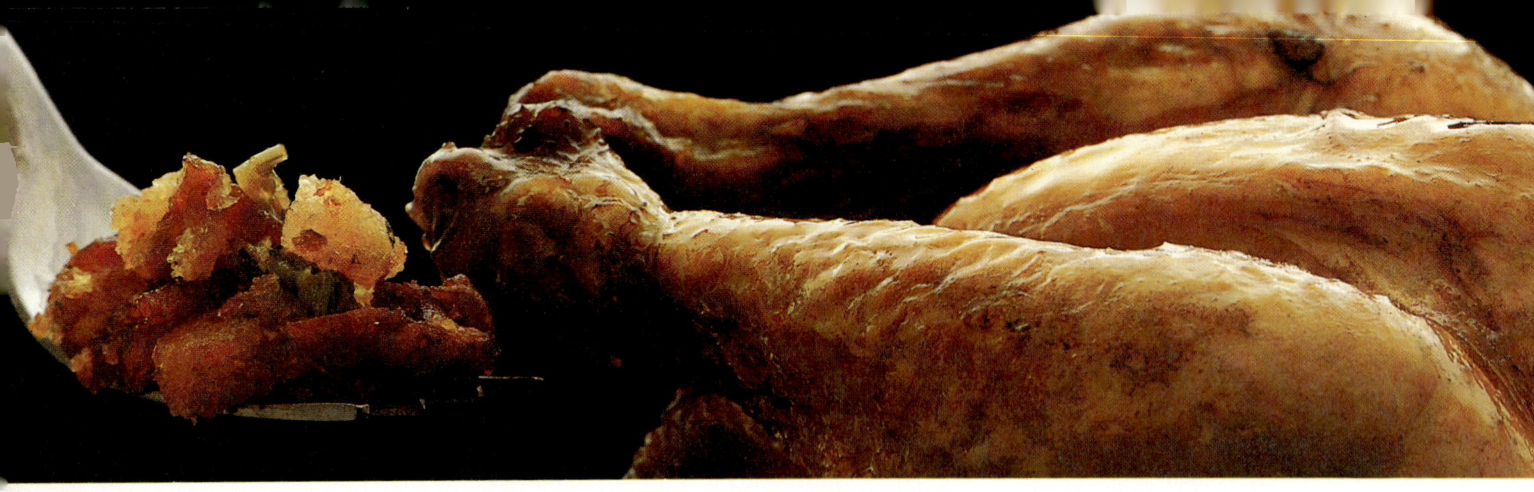

◄ Cornish Hens With Brazil Nut Stuffing

¼ cup chopped onion
⅓ cup thinly sliced celery
3 tablespoons butter or margarine
⅓ cup water
⅓ cup chopped Brazil nuts
1 cup herb-seasoned stuffing mix
2 Cornish game hens, giblets removed
2 teaspoons butter or margarine
2 teaspoons bouquet sauce

Serves 2 to 4

In 1-qt. measure combine onion, celery and butter. Microwave at High 2½ to 4 minutes, or until vegetables are tender.

In 1-cup measure, microwave water at High 45 seconds to 1½ minutes, or until boiling. Add to vegetable mixture. Stir in nuts and stuffing until evenly moistened. Stuff hens with mixture. Place breast side down on roasting rack in baking dish.

In custard cup melt butter at High 30 to 45 seconds. Stir in bouquet sauce. Brush hens with half of mixture. Cover with wax paper. Microwave at High 6 to 8 minutes, rotating dish after half the cooking time.

Turn hens over, brush with remaining mixture. Microwave 6 to 8 minutes, or until juices run clear and legs move easily, rotating dish once.

Microwave	15¾-22¼ min.

Bacon-Stuffed ▲ Cornish Hens

5 slices bacon, diced
¼ cup chopped onion
¼ cup thinly sliced celery
⅔ cup seasoned stuffing mix
1 teaspoon parsley flakes
¼ teaspoon salt
⅛ teaspoon pepper
2 Cornish game hens
1 tablespoon butter or margarine
2 teaspoons bouquet sauce

Serves 2

In 1-qt. casserole microwave bacon at High 4 to 5 minutes or until crisp. Remove to paper towels. Drain fat, reserving 3 tablespoons. Add onion and celery to fat in casserole. Microwave at High 2 to 4 minutes, or until tender. Stir in bacon, stuffing mix, parsley flakes, salt and pepper. Fill hens with stuffing. Place breast side down on roasting rack. Set aside.

In 1-cup measure, melt butter at High 30 to 60 seconds. Blend in bouquet sauce. Brush hens with one-fourth of mixture. Cover with wax paper. Microwave at High 8 minutes. Turn over; brush with remaining mixture. Cover. Microwave at High 7½ to 9½ minutes, or until legs move freely and juices run clear. Let stand tented 5 minutes.

Microwave	22-27½ min.
Standing	5 min.

Cranberry Cornish Hens

- 1 can (8 oz.) whole cranberry sauce
- 1 tablespoon orange juice
- 1 teaspoon sugar
- ½ teaspoon grated orange peel
- 3 tablespoons butter or margarine
- ¼ cup hot water
- 1½ cups plain dry bread cubes
- ¼ cup chopped pecans
- 2 tablespoons raisins
- ¼ teaspoon salt
- ⅛ teaspoon cinnamon
- Dash pepper
- 2 Cornish game hens (1 to 1½ lbs. each)
- 1 teaspoon butter or margarine
- 1 teaspoon bouquet sauce

Serves 2

Microwave 17¼-25½ min.

How to Microwave Cranberry Cornish Hens

Combine cranberry sauce, orange juice, sugar and orange peel in 2-cup measure. Microwave at High 1 to 2 minutes, or until heated. Set aside. In medium bowl melt 3 tablespoons butter at High 1 minute.

Stir in water, bread cubes, pecans, raisins, salt, cinnamon, pepper and one-fourth of the cranberry sauce. Use to stuff hens. Place hens breast side down on roasting rack.

Melt 1 teaspoon butter in custard cup at High 15 to 30 seconds. Stir in bouquet sauce. Brush hens with half of the mixture. Cover with wax paper.

Microwave at High 10 minutes. Rearrange hens and turn over. Brush with remaining bouquet sauce. Re-cover. Microwave at High 4 to 11 minutes, or until legs move freely and juices run clear.

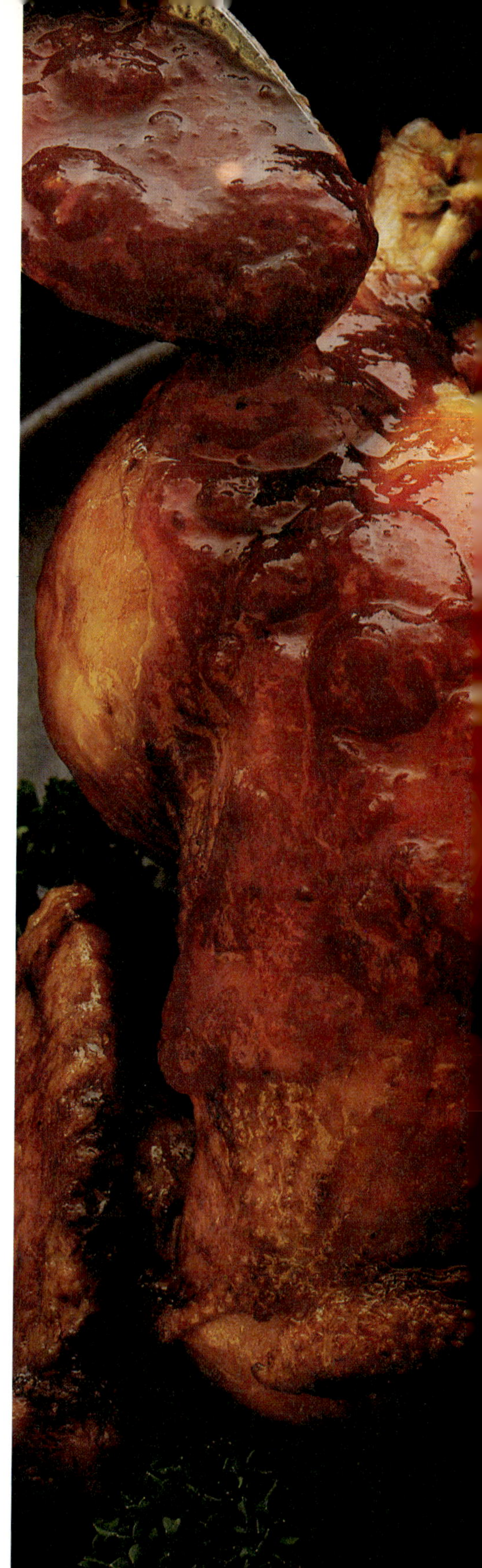

Reheat remaining cranberry mixture at High 1 minute, or until hot. Serve with hens and stuffing.

Dutch Omelet

1 small onion, chopped
½ lb. ground pork sausage
2 cups shredded potatoes
¾ teaspoon salt, divided
6 eggs
¼ cup milk
⅛ teaspoon pepper
Dash cayenne pepper

Serves 4

Microwave	18½-28 min.
Standing	2 min.

How to Microwave Dutch Omelet

Place onion and sausage in 2-qt. casserole. Microwave at High 3½ to 5 minutes, or until sausage loses its pink color, stirring once or twice.

Remove sausage and onion to paper towels. Discard all but 1 tablespoon fat from casserole.

Add potatoes to casserole. Cover. Microwave 4 to 6 minutes, or until tender. Sprinkle ¼ teaspoon salt over potatoes and stir to coat.

Combine eggs, ½ teaspoon salt, milk, pepper and cayenne. Pour over potatoes. Sprinkle sausage mixture on top. Microwave uncovered 3 minutes.

Lift edges with spatula so uncooked portion spreads evenly, taking care not to disrupt potatoes. Reduce power to 50% (Medium).

Microwave 8 to 14 minutes, or until eggs are almost set, rotating dish twice during cooking. Let stand loosely tented with foil 2 minutes before serving.

Egg Foo Yung

- 1 cup water
- 1 tablespoon cornstarch
- 1 tablespoon soy sauce
- 2 teaspoons instant chicken bouillon granules
- 1 teaspoon sugar
- Dash ginger
- 3 green onions chopped
- ½ medium green pepper, chopped
- 1 tablespoon butter or margarine
- 6 eggs, well beaten
- 1 can (16 oz.) bean sprouts, drained
- ½ teaspoon salt

Serves 4

Variation:
Add 1 can (4½ oz.) tiny shrimp, drained, with the bean sprouts. Microwave at 50% (Medium) 2½ to 3½ minutes longer.

Microwave 17-24 min.

How to Microwave Egg Foo Yung

Combine water, cornstarch, soy sauce, chicken bouillon, sugar and ginger in 1-qt. measure. Microwave at High 3½ to 5 minutes, or until thickened, stirring twice. Let stand while preparing eggs.

Place onion, green pepper and butter in 2-qt. casserole. Microwave at High 3½ to 5 minutes, or until green pepper is tender-crisp, stirring after half the time. Add beaten eggs, bean sprouts and salt to green pepper and onion.

Microwave 3 minutes. Stir to break up; push cooked portions to center. Reduce power to 50% (Medium). Microwave 7 to 11 minutes, or until set, rotating dish ¼ turn twice during cooking. Pour sauce over eggs before serving.

Overnight Cheese Stratas

4 slices white bread
Butter or margarine
2 tablespoons finely chopped onion
2 cups shredded Swiss cheese
1 can (5⅓ oz.) evaporated milk
½ cup milk
3 eggs
1 teaspoon salt
½ teaspoon dry mustard
2 teaspoons parsley flakes

Serves 4

Variation:
Microwave ½ lb. ground pork sausage at High 2½ to 4 minutes, or until meat loses its pink color. Crumble and drain. Add with onion and cheese.

Microwave	18-26 min.
Standing	3 min.

How to Microwave Overnight Cheese Stratas

Assemble the night before and microwave the next day. Butter one side of each slice of bread. Place slices buttered side down, in four individual casseroles. Top with onion and cheese.

Combine remaining ingredients except parsley flakes. Pour one fourth of mixture over each slice of bread. Top each casserole with ½ teaspoon parsley flakes. Cover; refrigerate overnight.

Microwave uncovered at 50% (Medium) 18 to 26 minutes, or until set, rearranging dishes twice during cooking. Let stand 3 minutes.

Meal Complements

Starches & Vegetables

Starches and vegetables are essential to good nutrition. If you're very pressed for time, serve bread as a starch and a mixed green salad as the vegetable. When you have more time, microwave instant potatoes or rice, and one of these vegetable recipes. Regular rice and pasta take time to rehydrate, even in a microwave oven. You can cook them conventionally while you microwave the main dish and vegetable.

Quick-Cooking Rice

Serves 4

Measure rice and salt into 2-qt. casserole, using proportions on package. Stir in hot water. Cover. Microwave at High 6 to 8 minutes, or until water is absorbed and rice is tender. Stir; let stand covered 2 to 4 minutes.

Microwave	6-8 min.
Standing	2-4 min.

Instant Mashed Potatoes

Serves 6

Combine water, milk, butter and salt in 4-cup measure, using proportions on package. Microwave at High 4 to 7 minutes, or until mixture just begins to boil. Stir in potato flakes.

To reheat: microwave at High 3½ to 5½ minutes, or until hot, stirring after half the time.

Microwave	4-7 min.

Baked Potatoes

Prick well-scrubbed potatoes twice. Place 1 inch apart in oven. Microwave at High; rearrange and turn over after half the time. Potatoes will feel slightly firm. Wrap in foil; let stand at least 5 minutes to complete cooking.

Medium Baking Potatoes	
1 potato	3-5 min.
2 potatoes	5-7½ min.
4 potatoes	10½-12½ min.

Twice Baked Potatoes

2 medium baking potatoes
⅓ cup milk
¼ cup salad dressing or mayonnaise
1 tablespoon butter or margarine
Salt
Pepper
1 teaspoon chopped chives

Serves 4

Microwave potatoes and let stand as directed on page 132. Slice each potato in half lengthwise. Scoop out center. Mash with milk, dressing, butter, salt and pepper. Spoon into shells. Sprinkle with chives.

Before serving, reheat at High 1½ to 3 minutes; rearrange once.

Potatoes may be prepared the night before. Add 1 to 2 minutes to reheating time.

Microwave	6½-10½ min.
Standing	5-10 min.

Bacon-Cheese Stuffed Potatoes

4 medium baking potatoes
6 slices bacon
½ cup milk
3 tablespoons butter or margarine
¼ teaspoon salt
½ teaspoon dry mustard
⅛ teaspoon pepper
⅔ cup shredded Cheddar or American cheese
1 teaspoon chives

Serves 4

Microwave potatoes as directed on page 132. While potatoes are standing, microwave bacon.

Place bacon on 2 layers of paper towels. Cover with 2 more layers of towels. Microwave at High 4 to 4½ minutes, or until slightly underdone. Let stand while preparing potatoes.

Slice top from each potato. Scoop out center and place in medium mixing bowl. Set shells aside. Add milk, butter and seasonings to potato. Mash until fluffy. Stir in cheese.

Crumble bacon; add two-thirds of it to potato mixture. Spoon mixture into potato shells. Sprinkle remaining bacon and chives over top.

Place stuffed potatoes on serving plate. Microwave at High 3 to 4 minutes, or until hot, rotating dish ½ turn after half the cooking time.

Microwave	17½-21 min.
Standing	5-10 min.

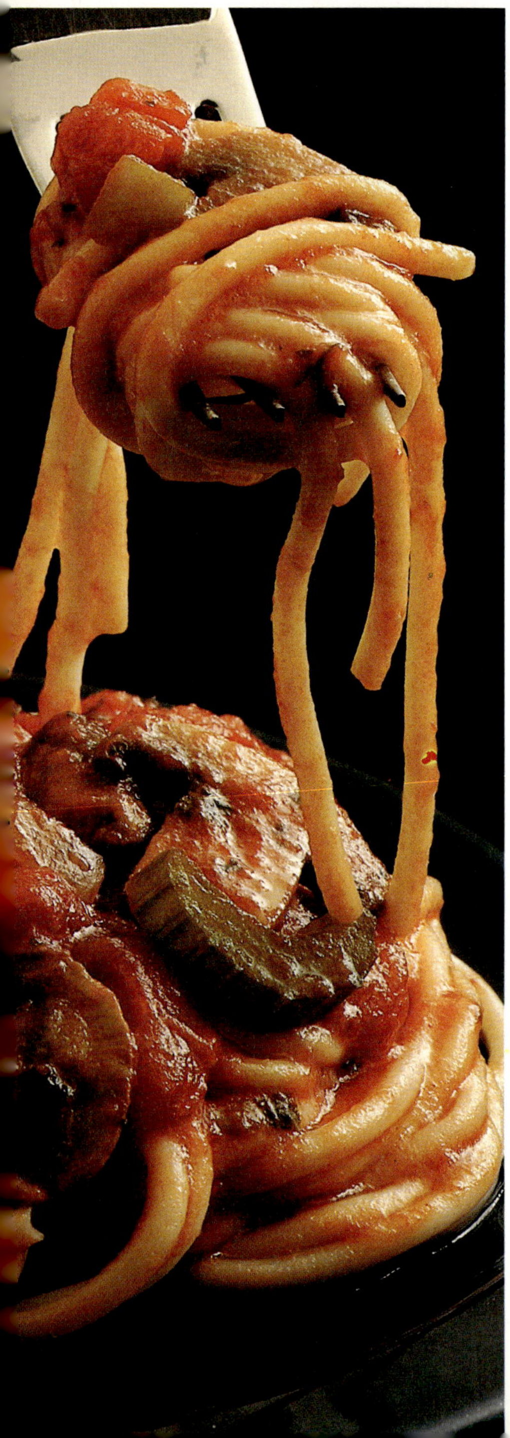

◂ Mushroom Spaghetti

4 servings spaghetti
1 lb. fresh mushrooms, sliced
1 stalk celery, chopped
1 small onion, chopped
¼ cup chopped green pepper
1 clove garlic, minced or pressed
2 tablespoons butter or margarine
1 can (16 oz.) stewed tomatoes, drained of ¼ cup liquid
1 can (6 oz.) tomato paste
2 teaspoons parsley flakes
1 teaspoon sugar
1 teaspoon salt
½ teaspoon basil
½ teaspoon oregano
⅛ teaspoon pepper

Serves 4

Cook spaghetti conventionally while microwaving sauce. In 2-qt. casserole combine mushrooms, celery, onion, green pepper, garlic and butter. Cover. Microwave at High 4 to 5 minutes, or until vegetables are tender.

Stir in remaining ingredients. Cover. Microwave 5 minutes. Reduce power to 50% (Medium). Microwave uncovered 17 to 20 minutes, or until sauce is thickened, stirring at least once during cooking. Serve over hot spaghetti.

Microwave	26-30 min.

Scalloped Hash Browns ▴

¼ cup chopped green onion, tops included or 1 tablespoon freeze-dried chopped chives
1 tablespoon butter or margarine
3 cups loose frozen hash browns
1 can (10¾ oz.) cream of chicken soup
1 cup shredded Cheddar cheese
½ cup sour cream
½ teaspoon salt
⅛ teaspoon pepper
½ cup crushed cheese crackers

Serves 4 to 6

Place onion and butter in 8×8-in. dish. Cover with wax paper. Microwave at High 1½ to 2 minutes, or until onion is tender.

Stir in remaining ingredients except cracker crumbs. Cover with wax paper. Microwave at High 8 to 9 minutes, or until cheese melts and potatoes are tender, stirring 3 or 4 times during cooking.

Sprinkle with cracker crumbs. Microwave uncovered 2 minutes, or until thoroughly heated.

Microwave	11½-13 min.

Snapped Up Green Beans ►

1 pkg. (9 oz.) frozen French style green beans
4 slices bacon, cut into ¾-in. pieces
¼ cup chopped onion
1 tablespoon vinegar
2 teaspoons water
2 teaspoons sugar
¼ teaspoon salt
Dash pepper

Serves 4

Defrost green beans in package at High 2½ to 3 minutes. Drain.

In 1-qt. casserole combine bacon and onion. Cover with wax paper. Microwave at High 4 to 5 minutes, or until bacon is crisp. Drain all but 1 tablespoon fat.

Add beans and remaining ingredients. Re-cover. Microwave at High 2 to 2½ minutes, or until green beans are tender, stirring after half the time.

Defrost	2½-3 min.
Microwave	6-7½ min.

Harvard Beets ►

3 tablespoons sugar
1 tablespoon cornstarch
¼ teaspoon salt
Dash pepper
2 cans (16 oz.) sliced beets, drained and ½ cup liquid reserved
3 tablespoons vinegar

Serves 4

In 1-qt. casserole combine sugar, cornstarch and seasonings. Stir in reserved beet liquid and vinegar. Microwave at High 3 minutes, or until thickened, stirring after every minute.

Mix in beets. Microwave at High 2½ to 3 minutes, or until heated through.

Microwave	5½-6 min.

Italian Brussels Sprouts

- 2 pkgs. (8 oz.) frozen Brussels sprouts
- 2 tablespoons water
- ¼ cup chopped green onion
- 2 tablespoons butter or margarine
- 2 teaspoons lemon juice
- ¼ teaspoon salt
- ⅛ teaspoon basil
- ⅛ teaspoon oregano
- Dash pepper

Serves 4 to 6

In 1½ to 2-qt. casserole combine Brussels sprouts and water. Cover; microwave at High 7 to 9 minutes, or until tender, stirring after half the cooking time. Set aside, covered.

Place green onion and butter in small bowl. Microwave at High 1½ to 2 minutes, or until onion is tender. Stir in remaining ingredients.

Drain Brussels sprouts. Pour onion mixture over sprouts. Stir to coat. Microwave at High 30 seconds to heat if needed.

Microwave 9-11½ min.

Cheesy Broccoli & Cauliflower

- 1 pkg. (10 oz.) frozen broccoli cuts
- 1 pkg. (10 oz.) frozen caulifloweret
- 2 tablespoons water
- ⅔ cup milk
- 1 envelope cheese sauce mix
- 2 tablespoons butter or margarine
- ⅓ cup fine dry bread crumbs

Serves 4 to 6

In 1½-qt. casserole combine broccoli, cauliflowerets and water. Cover. Microwave at High 10 to 12 minutes, or until tender, stirring once or twice to break up pieces. Drain well and return to covered casserole; set aside.

In 2-cup measure combine milk and cheese sauce mix. Microwave at High 2 to 3 minutes, or until thickened, stirring every minute. Set aside.

In small dish melt butter at High 15 to 30 seconds. Stir in bread crumbs. Pour cheese sauce over vegetables. Sprinkle with bread crumbs.

Microwave 12¼-15½ min.

Lightly Glazed Carrots

6 medium carrots, peeled and sliced ¼-in. thick
2 tablespoons water
¼ teaspoon salt
2 tablespoons brown sugar
1 tablespoon honey
2 teaspoons butter or margarine
½ teaspoon grated orange peel
½ teaspoon cornstarch

Serves 4

In 1½-qt. casserole combine carrots, water and salt. Cover. Microwave at High 7 to 8 minutes, or until tender, stirring after half the cooking time. Set aside.

In small bowl or 1-cup measure combine remaining ingredients. Microwave at High 45 to 60 seconds or until clear, thickened and bubbly, stirring once.

Drain carrots. Pour glaze over and toss to coat.

Microwave	7¾-9 min.

Caraway Cabbage

4 cups shredded green cabbage
2 tablespoons water
1 tablespoon butter or margarine
2 tablespoons cream
½ teaspoon salt
¼ teaspoon caraway seed
Dash pepper

Serves 4

In 2-qt. casserole combine cabbage, water and butter. Cover. Microwave at High 6 to 7 minutes or until tender. Drain.

Stir in remaining ingredients. Microwave at High 30 seconds to heat through.

Microwave	6½-7½ min.

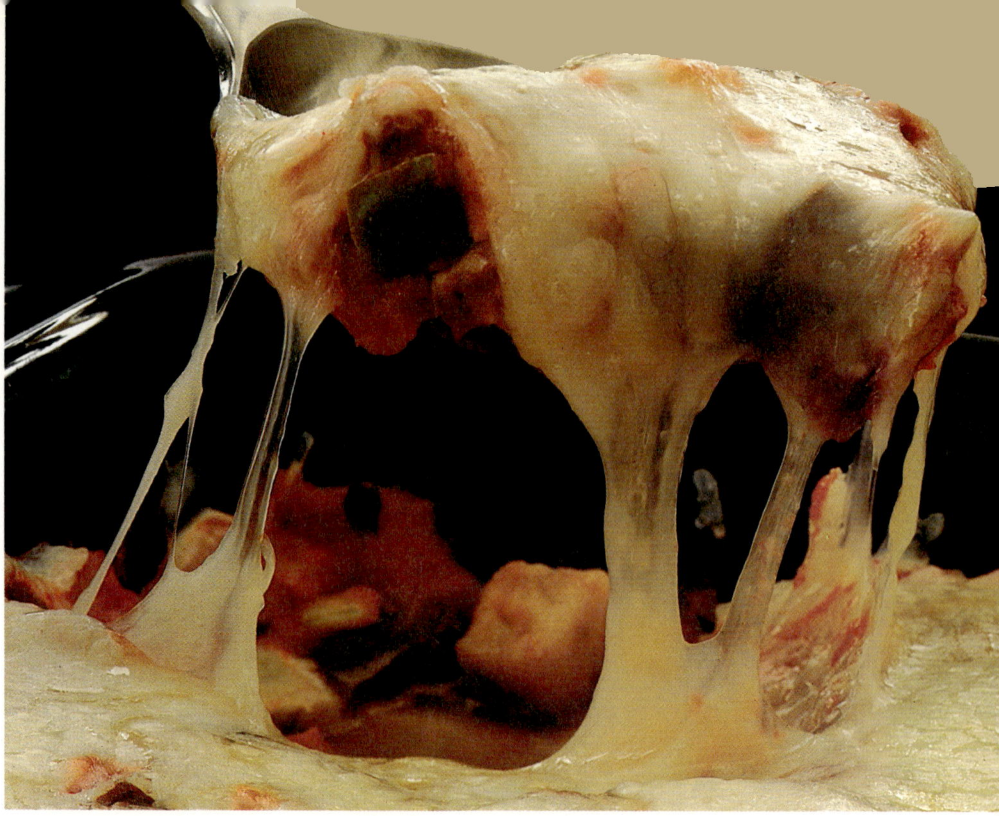

Riviera Eggplant Bake

1 medium onion, chopped
1/8 teaspoon garlic powder
1/2 cup chopped green pepper
1 tablespoon olive oil
1 can (6 oz.) tomato paste
1/2 cup tomato juice
2 teaspoons sugar
1/4 teaspoon oregano
1/4 teaspoon basil
1/8 teaspoon pepper
1 bay leaf
1 medium eggplant
8 oz. shredded mozzarella cheese, divided
1 tablespoon grated Parmesan cheese

Serves 4

Microwave 15 1/2-22 min.

How to Microwave Riviera Eggplant Bake

Combine onion, garlic, green pepper and olive oil in 2-qt. casserole. Microwave at High 2 1/2 to 3 minutes or until tender.

Stir in tomato paste, tomato juice, sugar and seasonings. Microwave at High 3 to 6 minutes, or until bubbly, stirring once during cooking. Set aside.

Cut eggplant into 1/2-in. cubes while microwaving sauce. Arrange cubes in 8×8-in. dish.

Cover with wax paper; microwave at High 6 to 8 minutes, or until tender and translucent.

Sprinkle half the mozzarella over eggplant. Spoon on sauce. Top with remaining mozzarella and Parmesan cheese.

Microwave at High 4 to 5 minutes, or until cheese melts, rotating dish 1/2 turn after half the cooking time.

Creamed Spinach

1 pkg. (10 oz.) frozen chopped spinach
1 tablespoon butter or margarine
1 tablespoon flour
¼ teaspoon sugar
¼ teaspoon salt
⅛ teaspoon nutmeg
Dash pepper
½ cup light cream

Serves 4

Place spinach in 1-qt. casserole. Cover; microwave at High 6 to 7 minutes, or until tender, stirring after half the time. Set aside.

In 1-cup measure, melt butter at High 15 to 30 seconds. Stir in flour, sugar and seasonings. Blend in cream. Microwave at High 1½ to 2 minutes, or until thickened, stirring once.

Drain spinach. Pour on thickened sauce and toss to coat.

Microwave 7¾-9½ min.

Peas, Onions & Mushrooms

1 small onion, thinly sliced
1 tablespoon butter or margarine
1 pkg. (10 oz.) frozen peas
1 can (4 oz.) mushroom stems and pieces, drained
½ teaspoon salt
¼ teaspoon chervil
Dash pepper

Serves 4

Place onion and butter in 1-qt. casserole. Cover. Microwave at High 1½ to 2 minutes, or until onion is tender.

Stir in remaining ingredients. Cover. Microwave at High 5 to 6 minutes, or until peas are heated thoroughly, stirring after half the cooking time.

Microwave 6½-8 min.

Zucchini Parmesan

3 cups zucchini cut into ¼-in. slices
1 tablespoon butter or margarine
1½ to 2 tablespoons grated Parmesan cheese
1 teaspoon parsley flakes
Dash salt
Dash pepper

Serves 4

Arrange zucchini slices in 8 to 9-in. round baking dish. Dot with butter. Cover with plastic wrap. Microwave at High 4 to 6 minutes or until tender-crisp. Drain.

Combine cheese, parsley flakes, salt and pepper. Sprinkle over zucchini before serving.

Microwave	4-6 min.

Zucchini & Tomatoes

2 cups thinly sliced zucchini
½ teaspoon basil leaves
1 teaspoon butter or margarine
1½ cups coarsely chopped tomatoes
½ teaspoon salt
Parmesan cheese

Serves 4

In 1-qt. casserole combine zucchini, basil and butter. Cover. Microwave at High 2 minutes. Stir in tomatoes and salt. Cover. Microwave at High 2 to 4 minutes, or until zucchini is tender. Sprinkle with Parmesan cheese. Let stand covered 2 to 5 minutes, or until cheese melts.

Microwave	4-6 min.
Standing	2-5 min.

Stir-Fried Vegetables

3 tablespoons soy sauce
1 teaspoon cornstarch
¼ teaspoon sugar
4 cups small caulifowerets
2 cups sliced fresh mushrooms
⅓ cup sliced green onions (tops included)
¼ cup slivered almonds
1 tablespoon butter or margarine

Serves 4

Variations:
Substitute 1 lb. fresh asparagus, cleaned and cut into 1½-in. pieces, or 4 cups fresh broccoli flowerets for cauliflower.

Microwave	9-12 min.

How to Microwave Stir-Fried Vegetables

Combine soy sauce, cornstarch and sugar in medium bowl. Stir in vegetables and almonds. Let stand while preheating browning dish.

Preheat browning dish at High 3 minutes. Add butter and tilt dish to coat bottom. Stir in vegetable mixture. Cover.

Microwave at High 6 to 9 minutes or until cauliflower is tender-crisp, stirring after half the time.

Vegetable Chart

Microwave vegetables at High in a covered dish. Covering holds in steam to tenderize food, keep it moist and shorten cooking time. Plastic wrap can be used for dishes which do not have covers.

Vegetable	Amount	Microwave Time, Minutes	Standing Time, Covered, Minutes	Procedure
Artichokes				
Fresh	2	5½-8½ min.	3 min.	Trim and rinse artichokes. Wrap in plastic wrap. Arrange in oven with spaces between.
	4	9½-14½ min.	3 min.	
Frozen	9 oz. pkg.	5-6 min.	2 min	1-qt. casserole. 2 tablespoons water. Stir, break apart after 2 min.
Asparagus				
Fresh	1 lb.	6½-9½ min.	3 min.	12×8-in. dish. ¼ cup water. Rearrange after 4 min.
Frozen	10 oz. pkg.	5-7 min.	3 min.	1-qt. casserole. 2 tablespoons water. Stir once.
Canned spears & cut	15 oz. can	2-4 min.		1-qt. casserole. Drain all but 1 tablespoon liquid. Stir once.
Beans				
Fresh, Green & Wax	1 lb.	7-13½ min.	3 min.	Cut into 1½-in. pieces. 1½-qt. casserole. ¼ cup water. Stir once.
Frozen, Green	9 oz. pkg.	4-7 min.	3 min.	1-qt. casserole. 2 tablespoons water. Stir once.
Frozen, Lima	10 oz. can	4-7 min.		1-qt. casserole. 2 tablespoons water. Stir once.
Canned, Green & Wax	15½ oz. can	2-4 min.		1-qt. casserole. Drain all but 2 tablespoons liquid. Stir once.
Canned, Lima	15-16 oz. can	2-3 min.	1 min.	1-qt. casserole. Drain all but 2 tablespoons liquid. Stir once.
Canned, Pork & Beans	16 oz. can	3-4 min.		1-qt. casserole. Stir after first 2 min.
Beets				
Canned	16 oz. can	2-3 min.		1-qt. casserole. Drain all but 2 tablespoons liquid.
Broccoli				
Fresh spears	1½ lbs.	8-12 min.	3 min.	12×8-in. dish. ½ cup water. Rotate dish ½ turn after half the cooking time.
Frozen	10 oz. pkg.	5-7 min.	3 min.	1-qt. casserole. 2 tablespoons water. Stir once after 2 min.
Brussels Sprouts				
Fresh	4 cups	4-8 min.	3 min.	1½-qt. casserole. ¼ cup water. Stir once.
Frozen	10 oz. pkg.	5-7 min.	3 min.	1-qt. casserole. 2 tablespoons water. Stir once.
Cabbage				
Shredded	1 lb.	7½-13½ min.	3 min.	¼-in. wide shreds. 1½-qt. casserole. 2 tablespoons water. Stir once.
Wedges	1 lb.	12½-15½ min.	2-3 min.	12×8-in. dish. ¼ cup water. Rearrange wedges and rotate dish after half cooking time.
Carrots				
Fresh, slices ⅛-in.	2 cups	4½-6½ min.	3 min.	1-qt. casserole. 2 tablespoons water. Stir once.
Fresh, shredded	2 cups	3½-6½ min.	2 min.	9-in. baking dish. 2 tablespoons butter. Stir once after butter melts.
Frozen, sliced	2 cups	4-7 min.	3 min.	1-qt. casserole. 2 tablespoons water. Stir once.
Cauliflower				
Fresh, flowerets	2 cups	5-7 min.	3 min.	1-qt. casserole. 2 tablespoons water. Stir once.
Fresh, whole	1 lb.	5½-7½ min.	3 min.	Wrap in plastic wrap. Turn over after 3 min.
Frozen	10 oz. pkg.	5-7 min.	3 min.	1-qt. casserole. 2 tablespoons water. Stir once.

Vegetable	Amount	Microwave Time, Minutes	Standing Time, Covered, Minutes	Procedure
Corn				
Fresh, Cob	2 ears 4 ears	7-10 min. 12-16 min.	5 min. 5 min.	8×8-in. or 12×8-in. dish. ¼ cup water. Turn over and rearrange once or twice.
Frozen, Cob	2 small ears	5½-7½ min.	3 min.	8×8-in. dish. 2 tablespoons water.
Frozen, whole kernel	10 oz. pkg.	4-6 min.	3 min.	1-qt. casserole. 2 tablespoons water. Stir once.
Canned, cut whole kernel	16 oz. can	2-3 min.		1-qt. casserole. Drain all but 2 tablespoons liquid. Stir once.
Mushrooms				
Fresh, sliced	½ lb.	3-6 min.	2 min.	8×8-in. dish. 2 tablespoons butter. Stir once.
Okra				
Frozen, sliced		5-7 min.	2 min.	1-qt. casserole. 2 tablespoons water. Stir at 2 min. intervals.
Frozen, whole		5-6 min.	2 min.	1-qt. casserole. 2 tablespoons water. Stir at 2 min. intervals.
Canned	14½ oz. can	3-4 min.		1-qt. casserole. Drain all but 2 tablespoons liquid. Stir once or twice.
Onions				
Fresh	2 whole 4 whole	6-8 min. 9-12 min.	1-2 min. 1-2 min.	Custard cups or baking dish. Rotate onions after half cooking time.
Peas, Black-eyed				
Frozen	10 oz. pkg.	8-9 min.	2 min.	1-qt. casserole. ¼ cup water. Stir at 2 min. intervals.
Peas, Green				
Fresh	2 cups	5-8 min.	3 min.	1-qt. casserole. ¼ cup water. Stir once.
Frozen	10 oz. pkg.	4-6 min.	3 min.	1-qt. casserole. 2 tablespoons water. Stir once.
Canned	16 oz. can	2-3 min.		1-qt. casserole. Drain all but 2 tablespoons liquid. Stir once.
Pea Pods				
Fresh	¼ lb.	2-4½ min.	2 min.	1-qt. casserole. 2 tablespoons water.
Frozen	6 oz. pkg.	3-4 min.	2 min.	1-qt. casserole. 2 tablespoons water. Stir once.
Potatoes				
Baked	2 4	5-7½ min. 10½-12½ min.	5-10 min. 5-10 min.	Prick potatoes. Place on paper towel. Turn over and rearrange after half cooking time. Let stand wrapped in foil.
Boiled	4 med.	9-12 min.	3 min.	Peel and quarter potatoes. 1 to 1½-qt. casserole. ¼ cup water. ½ teaspoon salt. Rearrange after half cooking time. Drain and slice.
Spinach				
Fresh	1 lb.	5-8 min.	3 min.	3-qt. casserole. 2 tablespoons water. Stir once.
Canned	15 oz. can	3-4 min.		1-qt. casserole. Drain all liquid. Stir once.
Squash				
Zucchini, fresh ¼-in. slices	2 cups	2½-6½ min.	3 min.	9-in. dish or 2-qt. casserole. 2 tablespoons butter or margarine. Stir once.
Acorn Squash, fresh (1½ lbs.)	1 2	8½-11½ min. 13-16 min.	5-10 min. 5-10 min.	Wrap each squash half with plastic wrap. Rotate and rearrange halves after half cooking time.
Frozen, mashed squash	12 oz.	5½-8 min.		1-qt. casserole. Break apart after 2 min., then stir at 2 min. intervals.
Sweet Potatoes				
Baked (5-7 oz.)	2 whole 4 whole	5-9 min. 8-13 min.	3 min. 3 min.	Wash, prick, place on paper towel. Rearrange once during cooking.
Tomatoes				
Fresh	2 4	1-3 min. 2½-4½ min.	2 min. 2 min.	Halve tomatoes. Round or rectangular dish.
Canned, stewed	14½ oz. can	3-5 min.		1-qt. casserole. Stir once.

Appetizers

The appetizers in this section are designed for those occasions when you want the meal itself to be festive and leisurely, even though you don't have much time to prepare it. The recipes on this page could be made at the last minute (they only take minutes), but they can be prepared several days in advance. Another short-cut idea is to mix dips and fillings in the morning, then refrigerate them until you are ready to assemble, microwave and serve. Appetizers aren't just for company meals. When the family is ready to eat, but the meal is not, serve an appetizer while you microwave the main dish.

Make-Ahead Cheese Nuggets

½ cup plus 1 tablespoon butter or margarine
1 teaspoon Worcestershire sauce
½ cup Parmesan cheese
4 cups spoon size shredded wheat
1 cup salted peanuts, optional

Makes 4 to 5 cups

In 3-qt. casserole microwave butter at High 1 to 2 minutes, or until melted. Blend in Worcestershire sauce and cheese. Stir in remaining ingredients to coat thoroughly. Microwave at 50% (Medium) 5 to 12 minutes, or until mixture browns slightly, stirring every 1 or 2 minutes. Turn out onto paper towels to absorb any excess oil. Store in airtight container.

Microwave 6-14 min.

Make-Ahead Piquant Pecans

6 tablespoons butter or margarine
2 tablespoons steak sauce
1 teaspoon soy sauce
10 dashes tabasco sauce
4 cups (about 1 lb.) pecan halves

Makes 4 cups

In 3-qt. casserole microwave butter at High 1 to 1½ minutes, or until melted. Blend sauces into the melted margarine. Add pecans and stir to coat well. Microwave at High 7 to 11 minutes, or until pecans are cooked. Drain off any remaining butter. Turn pecans out onto paper towel to absorb excess oil. Store in airtight containers.

Microwave 8-12½ min.

Cheese & Sausage Nuggets

1 cup buttermilk baking mix
1 cup grated sharp Cheddar cheese
1 egg, lightly beaten
6 oz. hot sausage
½ teaspoon bouquet sauce

Topping:
¼ cup seasoned bread crumbs
1 teaspoon ground oregano

Dip:
Mustard sauce

Makes about 4 dozen

Combine baking mix and cheese in medium bowl. Mix in egg, sausage and bouquet sauce. Shape mixture into 1-in. balls. Combine topping ingredients and coat balls with mixture. Place 9 or 12 balls, close together, in ring on large pie plate or dinner plate. Place 3 in center of ring. Microwave 1 to 2 minutes, until balls spring back when touched lightly, rotating ¼ turn after 1 minute, then every 30 seconds. Serve warm with mustard sauce.

Microwave 1-2 min.

Overnight Marinated Sweet & Sour Wings

2 lbs. chicken wings
½ cup brown sugar
¼ cup cider vinegar
2 tablespoons soy sauce
2 tablespoons catsup

Makes about 15 to 20

Cut off and discard wing tips and excess skin. Cut wings in half at joint. Place in 8×8-in. baking dish.

Combine sugar, vinegar, soy sauce and catsup. Pour over wings. Marinate 3 to 4 hours, or overnight in refrigerator, stirring once or twice to coat.

Microwave at High 11 to 22 minutes, or until fork tender when checked in several places, pushing center portions to outside of dish after half the time.

Microwave 11-22 min.

Crab Balls

1 can (6½ oz.) crab meat, rinsed,drained and flaked
1 egg, lightly beaten
2 tablespoons finely chopped green onion
1 teaspoon lemon juice
1 teaspoon Worcestershire sauce
2 tablespoons butter or margarine, melted
¼ teaspoon salt
⅛ teaspoon pepper
¾ cup flour
1 egg yolk
2 tablespoons milk

Topping:
2½ tablespoons plain bread crumbs
2½ tablespoons Parmesan cheese
2 teaspoons parsley flakes

Dip:
Cocktail Sauce

Makes about 30 balls

Combine all ingredients except egg yolk and milk in a medium bowl. Form into 1-in. balls.

Blend egg yolk and milk. Mix together topping ingredients in a small bowl. Dip balls into egg yolk mixture then roll in topping mixture to coat.

Arrange 10 to 12 close together in a ring around outside of large pie plate or dinner plate. Place 3 or 4 in center of ring.

Microwave at High 1 to 2½ minutes, or until balls are just firm, rotating ¼ turn after 1 minute, then every 30 seconds. Serve warm with cocktail sauce.

Microwave	1-1½ min.

Hot Florentine Dip

- 8 oz. cream cheese
- 2 tablespoons milk
- 1½ tablespoons minced onion
- ¾ teaspoon garlic salt
- ½ teaspoon black pepper
- 1 pkg. (10 oz.) frozen, chopped spinach
- 1 can (6¾ oz.) chunk ham, drained*
- 1 cup sour cream
- ¾ cup (about 3 oz.) chopped pecans, optional

Makes 3 cups

Microwave cream cheese in 2-qt. casserole at High for 30 seconds. Add seasonings and milk to cheese and cream together.

Place package of spinach on plate; microwave at High 5 to 6 minutes, or until defrosted, rotating ½ turn after 3 minutes. Drain spinach thoroughly.

Stir ham and spinach into cheese mixture. Fold in sour cream and pecans. Microwave at High 4 to 6 minutes, or until very hot, stirring gently after 2 minutes, then every minute. Place casserole on candle warmer or warming tray and serve with crackers.

*1 can (8½ oz.) small shrimp, drained, may be substituted for ham.

Microwave	9½-12½ min.

Rarebit Appetizer

- 1 can (10¾ oz.) cream of mushroom soup
- 2 tablespoons milk
- ½ teaspoon onion powder
- ½ teaspoon garlic powder
- ½ cup grated American cheese
- 2 cups grated, sharp Cheddar cheese
- ¼ cup white wine
- French bread cubes, raw vegetables, or sliced apples

Makes 2½ cups

Combine soup and milk in 2-qt. casserole. Microwave at High 2 to 3 minutes, or until very hot but not boiling, stirring every minute. Stir in seasonings, cheese, and wine. Microwave at High 2 to 6 minutes, or until cheese melts and mixture is hot and smooth, stirring every minute.

Place casserole over candle warmer or on warming plate and serve with French bread cubes, vegetables or sliced apples.

Microwave	4-9 min.

Cheesy Tomato Puffs

¼ to ⅓ lb. bacon, cut into ¼-in. widths
8 oz. cream cheese
½ teaspoon minced onion
1 teaspoon baking powder
1 egg yolk
⅓ cup finely chopped green pepper
2 to 3 pints firm cherry tomatoes

Makes about 50 puffs

Microwave	10½-11½ min.

How to Microwave Cheesy Tomato Puffs

Microwave bacon in 2-qt. covered casserole at High 9 minutes, or until crispy, stirring every 3 minutes. Drain well.

Place cream cheese in casserole with bacon; microwave at High 30 seconds to soften. Add onion, baking powder and egg yolk to cheese and bacon. With electric mixer, cream contents of casserole until well blended and fluffy. Stir in green pepper.

Cut tops from tomatoes and scoop out seeds. Fill with cheese mixture. Place 10 to 12 close together in ring on large dinner or pie plate lined with paper towel. Place 3 or 4 in center of ring.

Microwave at 50% (Medium) 1 to 2 minutes, or until cheese is just dry on surface, rotating ¼ turn every 30 seconds. Serve warm.

Desserts

For many people, a meal is not complete without dessert. Some of the recipes in this section can be microwaved while the family is eating dinner, so you can spend a full 30 minutes on the meal and serve a dessert, too. Other time savers are quick-to-microwave instant puddings or fruits, either fresh, frozen or canned. Many of the most popular desserts, like brownies, are served cool; they can't be prepared just before dinner, but take only minutes to microwave the night before.

◄ Mint Chocolate Sauce

16 chocolate covered mint patties (6 oz.)
¼ cup chocolate syrup
2 tablespoons half and half

Makes about ⅔ cup

Combine all ingredients in 2-cup measure. Microwave at High 1 to 2½ minutes, or until candies melt when stirred; stir once during cooking. Serve with ice cream or pound cake.

Microwave 1-2½ min.

Strawberry Sauce

2 tablespoons strawberry jam
½ teaspoon lemon juice
1 cup fresh sliced strawberries

Makes about 1 cup

In small bowl microwave jam at High 10 to 30 seconds to soften. Do not overheat. Stir in lemon juice and strawberries.

Serve over cheesecake or ice cream.

Microwave 10-30 sec.

Lemon-Orange Sauce

1 can (21 oz.) lemon pie filling
1 can (15 oz.) mandarin orange sections, juice drained and reserved
¼ cup Grand Marnier or Curacao and ⅓ cup reserved juice, or 1½ teaspoons orange extract and ⅔ cup reserved juice

Makes about 3 cups

Combine all ingredients in 1-qt. measure. Microwave at High 2 to 4 minutes, or until thoroughly heated, stirring once. Serve over angel food cake.

Microwave 2-4 min.

Peanut Butter Chocolate Sauce

½ cup chocolate chips
⅔ cup peanut butter chips
¼ cup half and half

Makes 1 cup

Combine all ingredients in small bowl or 2-cup measure. Microwave at High 1 to 3 minutes, or until chips are softened. Stir until smooth. Serve over ice cream or pound cake.

Variation:
Substitute butterscotch chips for peanut butter chips.

Microwave 1-3 min.

How To Defrost Frozen Desserts

	Power Level	Time
Pound Cake	High	1-1½ min.
Cheesecake	30% (Low)	3-4 min.
Cakes & Brownies	30% (Low)	1½-3½ min. per lb.
Cream Pies	30% (Low)	¾-2 min. per lb.

Remove from foil pan. Place on plate or pie pan. Microwave as directed above, rotating after half the time. Test by inserting wooden pick in center. Pick should meet little or no resistance. Let stand 2 to 5 minutes.

Cherry Almond Torte

1 can (21 oz.) cherry pie filling
2 teaspoons almond extract or ¼ cup Amaretto
1 frozen pound cake (10¾ oz.), sliced lengthwise into thirds
3 tablespoons sliced almonds

Serves 6

In medium bowl combine pie filling and almond extract. Place bottom third of pound cake on serving plate or in 8×8×3-in. loaf pan. Spoon one-third of fruit mixture onto cake, then sprinkle with 1 tablespoon almond slices. Repeat sequence with remaining layers. Microwave at High 3 to 4 minutes, or until thoroughly heated.

Variation:
Substitute 1 jar (14 oz.) cranberry-orange relish, 3 tablespoons strawberry preserves, and 2 teaspoons lemon juice for the cherry-almond filling. Add ¼ cup chopped pecans, if desired.

Microwave 3-4 min.

Hot Fruit Compote

2 cups frozen peaches (about one-half 16 oz. bag)
1 can (16 oz.) sliced pears, drained
1 can (13½ oz.) pineapple chunks, drained
1 cup seedless green grapes
½ cup coconut
¼ cup raisins
10 maraschino cherries
2 tablespoons brown sugar
⅛ teaspoon cinnamon
1 can (11 oz.) mandarin orange segments, drained
1 cup miniature marshmallows

Serves 6

Place frozen peaches in 2-qt. casserole. Microwave at High 1½ to 2 minutes, or until partially defrosted, stirring after half the time.

Stir in remaining ingredients, except orange segments and marshmallows. Microwave at High 5 to 6 minutes, or until thoroughly heated. Stir in orange segments and marshmallows. Serve.

Microwave 6½-8 min.

Overnight Ice Cream Pies

Graham Cracker Crust:
5 tablespoons butter or margarine
1⅓ cups fine graham cracker crumbs
2 tablespoons white or brown sugar

Makes 9-in. pie

Microwave 2¾-3½ min.

Pumpkin Ice Cream Pie:
1 qt. vanilla ice cream
1 cup canned pumpkin
½ cup packed brown sugar
1 teaspoon cinnamon
¼ teaspoon nutmeg
¼ teaspoon ginger

Combine flavorings in medium bowl. Prepare pie following photo directions. If desired, top with chopped walnuts or pecans.

Rocky Road Ice Cream Pie:
1 qt. chocolate ice cream
½ cup miniature chocolate chips
½ cup slivered almonds
2 cups miniature marshmallows

Prepare pie following photo directions, adding marshmallows after mixing in flavorings.

Creme de Menthe Ice Cream Pie:
1 qt. vanilla ice cream
¼ cup creme de menthe or creme de menthe syrup
2 to 3 drops green food coloring

Prepare pie following photo directions. If desired, top with Chocolate Mint Sauce.

Cranberry Ice Cream Pie:
1 qt. vanilla ice cream
1 pkg. (10 or 11 oz.) cranberry-orange relish

Prepare crust, substituting finely crushed lemon wafers or butter cookies for cracker crumbs, decreasing butter to ½ cup and omitting sugar. Prepare pie following photo directions.

How to Microwave Overnight Ice Cream Pies

Prepare crust. Melt butter in 9-in. pie plate at High 30 to 60 seconds. Stir in crumbs and sugar until well moistened. Press crumbs firmly and evenly against bottom and sides of plate. Microwave 1½ minutes, rotating ½ turn after 1 minute. Cool.

Place ice cream in large bowl. Divide into fourths. Microwave at 50% (Medium) 45 to 60 seconds, or until slightly softened. Do not let ice cream melt.

Mix in flavorings at lowest speed of electric mixer until well distributed. Spoon filling into pie shell. Freeze 2 hours or overnight until firm.

Index

D

E

F

N

O

P